Ksenija Ponomarenko
Anatolij Pudel'

Methods for ensuring security in big data (Big Data)

Ksenija Ponomarenko
Anatolij Pudel'

Methods for ensuring security in big data (Big Data)

banking sector

ScienciaScripts

Imprint
Any brand names and product names mentioned in this book are subject to trademark, brand or patent protection and are trademarks or registered trademarks of their respective holders. The use of brand names, product names, common names, trade names, product descriptions etc. even without a particular marking in this work is in no way to be construed to mean that such names may be regarded as unrestricted in respect of trademark and brand protection legislation and could thus be used by anyone.

Cover image: www.ingimage.com

This book is a translation from the original published under ISBN 978-620-8-01131-4.

Publisher:
Sciencia Scripts
is a trademark of
Dodo Books Indian Ocean Ltd. and OmniScriptum S.R.L publishing group

120 High Road, East Finchley, London, N2 9ED, United Kingdom
Str. Armeneasca 28/1, office 1, Chisinau MD-2012, Republic of Moldova, Europe
Printed at: see last page
ISBN: 978-620-8-12887-6

CONTENTS.

INTRODUCTION

In today's world, processing and analyzing large amounts of data is becoming an increasingly important task for various industries, including banking. Big Data, or Big Data, is information that is characterized by high speed of arrival, large volume and variety of sources, value and reliability

The very name "big data" refers to the substantial size of the data being processed. Big data is the huge "volumes" of data generated daily by many sources, such as business processes, machines, social media platforms, networks, human interaction, and more.

Big data can be structured, unstructured and semi-structured and can be collected from various data sources. Previously, data was accumulated only from databases and spreadsheets, but in modern times, data comes in completely different forms: PDF files, emails, audio files, electronic messages, digital photos, digital video streams, etc.

The total population of data can be classified according to their degree of ordering as follows:

- Structured data: in a structured schema along with all the necessary columns. Such data has a table form and is stored in a database management system;

- Semi-structured data: in semi-structured mode, the data schema is not properly defined. Examples of such data storage are JSON, XML, CSV, TSV and email file formats. OLTP (online transaction processing) systems are built to handle semi-structured data. It is stored in tabular form.

- Unstructured data: all unstructured files, log files, audio files and image files are included in unstructured data. Some organizations have a lot of data, but they do not know how to determine the value of the data because the data is raw.

- Quasi-structured data. Data format contains text data of inconsistent format, formatting of which requires effort and time.

Big data is also characterized by a number of properties:

Credibility is a property of data that enables efficient data processing and management.

Value is the most important characteristic of big data. Data value is a concept that describes the importance and usefulness of information that can be extracted from data. Data value can be defined in different ways depending on the context and objectives.

Velocity is the rate at which data is created in real time. It contains linking rates of incoming datasets, rates of change and bursts of activity. The main distinguishing aspect of big data is the need to provide the necessary data quickly.

The velocity of big data is related to the speed of data flows from sources: application logs, business processes, networks and social media sites, sensors, mobile devices, etc.

As the volume and importance of data grows, so do new security threats. Banking is one of the most vulnerable industries in this regard, as it contains a large amount of confidential customer information, financial transactions and commercial information. The loss or leakage of such information can lead to serious consequences, including financial losses, reputational damage and breach of legislation, and withdrawal of cooperation from key business partners.

The problems described above have a direct impact on the development of security solutions required to protect big data. However, due to the fact that information security is always a complex approach, there is no ready-made security solution that would meet the needs of every organization.

This paper will investigate security techniques in big data. Different security approaches such as data encryption, access control, authentication and auditing will be discussed. The advantages and disadvantages of the techniques and their applicability in the context of big data will be highlighted.

Attention will also be paid to the list of existing regulatory requirements and security standards in the banking sector of the Republic of Kazakhstan applicable to the processing of big data.

Based on the conducted research, a set of standards and recommendations for ensuring security in big data in the banking sector of the Republic of Kazakhstan will be developed. The main principles and approaches to ensuring security will be defined, and specific recommendations on application of these methods in the banking sphere will be offered.

A general testing approach will be described for the developed methods. The effectiveness criteria of big data security methods will be defined. The advantages and disadvantages of each method will be identified and their application areas will be defined.

The final chapter will describe the general approach to implementing the developed standards and recommendations in the banking sector of the Republic of Kazakhstan. Practical aspects of implementation will be discussed, such as the need for staff training, changes to existing processes and systems, and an assessment of the benefits of implementing these practices.

Thus, this paper aims to study and comparative analysis of methods of ensuring security in big data, as well as the development of standards and recommendations for their application in the banking sector of the Republic of Kazakhstan. The results of this study may be useful for organizations working with big data, especially in the banking sector, where data security is critical.

1 INTRODUCTION TO SECURITY ISSUES IN BIG DATA

1.1 Overview of methods for securing in big data

The modern world has witnessed an explosive growth in the amount of data generated and accumulated every day. This phenomenon, known as "big data" or "Big Data", represents a huge potential for various industries, including banking. Big Data can help banks make more informed decisions, improve customer service, detect fraudulent activity and much more. However, along with these opportunities come new challenges, especially in the area of data security [1].

Data security is one of the most important challenges faced by organizations dealing with big data. Given the volume and variety of data, as well as the speed at which it is processed, security in big data is becoming a challenge. Cybercriminals are constantly improving techniques to hack into systems and steal data, posing serious security threats to the banking industry. Companies and organizations must be prepared to protect data from various threats, including unauthorized access and modification of data, theft (leakage) of information, cyberattacks aimed at blocking access to data and other types of attacks [2].

One of the main problems in the field of data security in the banking sector of Kazakhstan is insufficient awareness and underestimation of risks inherent in information technologies by banking institutions. Many banks do not give due importance to data security, do not invest sufficient resources and do not develop effective information protection strategies. This is most often due to insufficient understanding of the level of impact on the organization's activities when information security risks are realized, and as a consequence, underestimation of the importance of allocating the necessary resources for data security, as well as the lack of qualified specialists in the field of information security. Repeated studies of the level of information security in the banking market of Kazakhstan confirm that even mature organizations with large IT budgets often do not pay due attention to the correct assessment of risks and configuration of information protection means [3].

There are more than seventy (70) legal acts and laws regulating the requirements for ensuring information security of the financial industry in Kazakhstan. A more detailed list of them is given in Table 1 to this study. At the same time, there is no single document accumulating all the necessary requirements to ensure information security when banks of the Republic of Kazakhstan use big data processing. Regulation of information security of banks in Kazakhstan consists of the requirements of laws and bylaws prepared by the following state bodies: the Agency of the Republic of Kazakhstan for Regulation and Development of Financial Market (hereinafter - ARDF), the National Bank of the Republic of Kazakhstan, the Ministry of Digital Development, Innovation and Aerospace Industry, the National Security Committee, the Ministry of Finance, the Agency of the Republic of Kazakhstan for Financial Monitoring, the Committee of the International Financial Center, and the Ministry of Finance. Such a wide regulatory field nevertheless has a weak implementation in banks due to limited resources allocated by the state to control compliance with the established requirements of information security. At the same time, it should be noted that the current administrative code of the Republic of Kazakhstan does not contain articles related to violation of information security requirements in the financial market. The main role in regulation of the financial market is played by the ARFM, in accordance with the mandate given by the Law of RK dated 04.07.2003. "The combination of these factors is a prerequisite for the current level of banks' vulnerability to cyberattacks.

Kazakhstan has a Law and bylaws aimed at protecting personal data, banking secrets, state secrets, commercial secrets and other types of secrets, while the regulatory acts do not emphasize the security requirements applied in the field of big data protection. The exception is the area of data management in public authorities and information systems belonging to them (the Order of the Minister of Digital Development, Innovation and Aerospace Industry No. 385/NK dated 14.10.2022 approved the "Requirements for Data Management") [4], which establishes the principles of data purity, defines the role model of participants processing data, and establishes upper-level data protection requirements. Among them we can mention:

- determining the degree of necessity of data protection depending on the class of data, which is assigned according to its scale, integrity and criticality, in accordance with the classifier of informatization objects;
- collection and analysis of data on the state of information security in the organization;
- risk assessment and planning of risk treatment measures in case of possible leakage (disclosure), distortion, deletion (loss) of data;
- realization and implementation of appropriate controls, assignment of roles and responsibilities, training of staff, operational work to implement protective measures;
- monitoring the functioning of controls, assessing their effectiveness and appropriate corrective actions;
- compliance with the requirements in the field of information and communication technologies and information security approved by the Government.

The concept of processing and collection of big data is in contradiction with one of the principles of information security "minimum sufficiency of authority", as well as difficult to be compatible with the principle of limiting the processing of personal data for predetermined purposes, established in the Law of the Republic of Kazakhstan "On personal data and their protection".

Currently, there are no significant fines that could force Big Data operators to implement security measures. For example, in the first quarter of 2024 in the financial sector there was a major leakage of a large database containing personal data of citizens of the Republic of Kazakhstan, which included data of two million people at the company "MFO "Robokash.kz" LLP, and in accordance with the current legislation the company incurred an insignificant fine of 1.8 million tenge. As a result, there is no motivation to invest in information security research and development. Some states are just beginning to think about writing laws to regulate big data. It is not yet clear how laws to protect personal data and other types of secrecy will affect laws to regulate the storage and processing of Big Data.

Within the framework of this paper we will investigate and compare different methods of ensuring security in the use of big data. Our goal is to develop standards and recommendations for the application of these methods in the banking sector of the Republic of Kazakhstan. Banks are a special sector where data security is of paramount importance. Leakage of customer information or fraudulent activity can lead to serious consequences for the bank and its customers. Therefore, it is necessary to develop effective methods to ensure security in big data, which take into account the specific requirements and regulatory features of the banking sector [5].

In this study, we will examine various aspects of security in big data, including protecting data at rest, during transmission, and during processing. We will also explore the different types of attacks that can target data and how to prevent them. Special attention will be paid to authentication and authorization mechanisms, data encryption, monitoring and anomaly detection, correct configuration of data processing hardware and software, and data access control [6].

One of the key aspects of security in big data is protection against unauthorized access. In banking, where data confidentiality and integrity are of particular importance, unauthorized access can lead to serious consequences. Therefore, when designing big data systems, it is important to use authentication and authorization mechanisms that will allow only the necessary list of users to access the data. This can be achieved through the use of strong passwords (such passwords are difficult to guess or pick), multi-factor authentication (an authentication method in which the user is asked to present at least two different types of evidence data: what the user has and what the user knows; what the user is), biometric methods, and other modern technologies.

Another important security aspect of big data processing is data encryption. Encryption helps protect data from unauthorized access, even if an attacker was able to gain physical access to the data storage. There are various encryption methods including symmetric and asymmetric encryption. Symmetric encryption uses the same key to encrypt and decrypt data, while asymmetric encryption uses a pair of keys - a public key and a private key. Both methods have their advantages and disadvantages, and the choice of method depends on the specific requirements and constraints.

Monitoring and anomaly detection also play an important role in big data security. Monitoring allows you to track data queries and identify suspicious activity that may indicate unauthorized access attempts or help identify data breaches that have occurred. Anomaly detection is based on analyzing data and identifying unusual or unexpected patterns. This can be accomplished by using statistical methods to detect certain patterns in event logs that capture data accesses, or by using machine learning and big data analytics. Monitoring and anomaly detection techniques can be effective tools to detect and prevent attacks and improve data protection.

Data access management is also an important aspect of security in big data. In banking, where data access can be divided into different levels and roles, it is important to have mechanisms that allow data access to be controlled based on the role and rights of the user. This can be achieved through Role Based Access Control, Mandate Based Access Control, Attribute Based Access Policies and other access control techniques.

In this paper we will investigate various methods of ensuring security in big data and compare their effectiveness and applicability in the banking sector of the Republic of Kazakhstan. We will also develop standards and recommendations for the application of these methods in the banking sector, which will help banks to increase the level of protection of their data and protect themselves from various threats to information security.

1.2 Relevance of the study of security in the banking sector of the Republic of Kazakhstan

The modern world is characterized by a huge amount of information that is generated and collected every second. Big Data has become an integral part of our lives and is used in various industries, including banking. However, as the volume and complexity of data grows, new challenges related to data security arise.

Banking sector is one of the most critical and important sectors of any country's economy, including the Republic of Kazakhstan. Banks store huge amounts of confidential information about their customers, including personal data, financial transactions, transaction history, etc.

This information is a valuable asset and can be used by criminals for fraud, identity theft and other criminal activities.

With the development of technology and the emergence of big data, the banking industry has faced new security challenges. The volume and complexity of data has increased significantly, which requires new approaches and methods to ensure its protection. In addition, new threats have emerged, such as hacker attacks on database processing systems, internal threats using untrustworthy IT administrators, accidental or intentional data breaches, and others.

The situation in the Republic of Kazakhstan is no exception. The banking sector in the country is actively developing and using big data to improve its operations. However, data security remains an urgent problem. In CIS countries there are a number of factors that make this problem particularly important [7,8].

Firstly, the Republic of Kazakhstan is a developing economy and the banking sector plays an important role in its development. Banks are actively introducing new technologies and using big data to optimize their operations and improve the efficiency of their services. However, as the use of big data increases, so does the risk of its leakage or unauthorized access to it.

Second, Kazakhstan is a country with a developed information infrastructure, which increases the attack surface and makes it more vulnerable to cyberattacks. Cybercrime is becoming more widespread and sophisticated, and the banking sector is one of its main targets. The Republic of Kazakhstan is taking various measures to increase its resilience to cyberattacks, the Republic of Kazakhstan ranks 78 (seventy-eighth) out of 176 countries in the Global Cybersecurity Index [9].

Third, Kazakhstan is actively working on technological modernization of its banking system and implementation of new methodological principles of the financial system. This includes the use of cloud technologies, implementation of Open Banking principles, digital tender of data analytics and other innovative solutions. However, with the increasing use of such technologies, new security threats are emerging that require additional data protection measures. Thus, in report on the activities of the Agency of the Republic of Kazakhstan on Regulation and Development of the Financial Market for 2022 it is indicated that banks in Kazakhstan faced 91 (ninety-one) information security incidents during the year [10].

The relevance of the thesis "Research and comparative analysis of security methods in Big Data (Big Data) and development of recommendations for their application" is conditioned, among other things, by the constant need to modify methods of ensuring security and confidentiality of information in the field of banking services, due to the continuous improvement of attackers of their methods, technologies and level of training. With the growing volume of data and the use of new technologies such as Big Data, banks are facing threats from hackers, cybercriminals and internal intruders. The development of practical standards and recommendations will help banks to protect data more effectively, reduce the risks of leakage and unauthorized access, and improve compliance with legal requirements for the protection of personal and other sensitive data.

The object of research in the work "Research and comparative analysis of methods for ensuring security in big data (Big Data) and development of recommendations for their application" is the banking sector of the Republic of Kazakhstan, in which the use of big data is becoming more and more widespread. The subject of the study is practical standards and recommendations that can be developed to ensure security when working with big data in the banking sector of the Republic of Kazakhstan. Due to the growing volume and importance of data in the banking sector, it is necessary to develop effective methods and tools to ensure and protect information security, as well as to establish standards and recommendations for their application. This will allow banks of the Republic of Kazakhstan to confidently work with big data, minimize risks and ensure protection of confidentiality and integrity of their clients' data. The work is aimed at analyzing existing methods of ensuring security in the field of big data and developing standards and recommendations that can be applied in the banking sector of Kazakhstan to ensure security and protection of data confidentiality.

This paper will review the basic concepts and principles of data security and their importance for the banking sector, analyze the existing methods of data security and their applicability in the context of big data, review various methods and technologies used to ensure data security in large volumes, as well as applicability in the banking sector of the Republic of Kazakhstan, will offer specific recommendations and standards that can be used by banks to ensure data security in the conte

Data security in big data processing is an urgent and complex problem, especially in the banking sector. The Republic of Kazakhstan, with its developing economy and developed cyberinfrastructure, faces data security threats that require comprehensive data protection measures. The development of recommendations to ensure security in big data in the banking sector of the Republic of Kazakhstan will help in ensuring confidentiality and integrity of financial industry data, as well as reducing possible threats and losses.

1.3 Aims and objectives of the study

Data security is one of the main aspects of information security, especially in the banking industry. Banks process huge amounts of information about their customers, including personal data, financial information and other sensitive information [10]. Therefore, protecting customer data is a priority for banks [11].

However, ensuring security in big data is a complex task that requires special approaches and methods. First, big data is characterized by a high degree of heterogeneity and dynamism. It can be collected from a variety of sources, including social media, mobile devices, sensors, and other sources. This means that the data may have different formats and structures, which complicates their processing and analysis [12].

Second, big data is characterized by high volume and update rates. The volume of data can reach several petabytes and continue to grow. This requires the use of special technologies and infrastructure for data storage, transmission and processing. Moreover, data can be updated in real time, which requires fast processing and analysis [13].

Third, big data often contains sensitive information that can be used for illegal purposes such as fraud, identity theft and other crimes. Therefore, data security becomes a particularly important concern in the context of big data.

The objective of this paper is to investigate and comparatively analyze the security techniques in big data. To achieve this goal, various approaches and technologies used for data protection in big data will be considered. Their advantages and disadvantages will be analyzed, as well as the possibilities of their application in the banking sector of the Republic of Kazakhstan.

In order to achieve the objective, the following tasks will be accomplished:

1. study of the basic principles and concepts of security in big data. Basic aspects of data security such as confidentiality, integrity and availability will be discussed. The main security threats in big data processing and methods of their prevention will be analyzed.

2. analyze existing methods and technologies for ensuring security in big data. Different approaches to data security will be considered, including encryption, authentication, authorization, security monitoring and auditing. Their advantages and disadvantages will be analyzed, as well as their potential applications in the context of big data.

3. study of the application of security methods in the banking sector of the Republic of Kazakhstan. Features of the banking sphere in the Republic of Kazakhstan and requirements to data security will be analyzed. Examples of application of security methods in the banking sector and their effectiveness will be considered.

4. Development of standards and recommendations on application of security methods in the banking sector of the Republic of Kazakhstan.

Based on the results of the research, recommendations on the application of security methods in the banking sector will be developed. Standards and recommendations on data protection in big data that can be used by banks in the Republic of Kazakhstan will be proposed.

Thus, this paper has an important practical significance, as the development of standards and recommendations for the application of security methods in big data in the banking sector of the Republic of Kazakhstan will improve the level of data security and protect the confidential information of customers.

2 METHODS FOR ENSURING SECURITY IN BIG DATA

2.1 Cryptographic methods for protecting data in large volumes

Big data security techniques play a critical role in today's information society. As the amount of data collected and processed by organizations continues to increase, it becomes increasingly important to protect it from unauthorized access, leaks, and misuse. Cryptographic methods of big data protection are one of the most effective ways to ensure security in such situations.

Cryptography is the science of methods to ensure confidentiality, integrity and authenticity of data using mathematical algorithms. It is a key tool in information security, and its application in big data is no exception. Cryptographic methods for protecting big data can ensure the confidentiality and integrity of information, as well as provide authenticity and continuity of data transmission.

One of the main cryptographic methods of data protection in large volumes is encryption [14]. Encryption is the process of transforming the original information into an unreadable form (ciphertext) using a special algorithm (cipher). Encryption allows data confidentiality, as only authorized users possessing the decryption key can read the data. Encryption can be symmetric or asymmetric.

Symmetric encryption involves using the same key to encrypt and decrypt data. This means that the sender and receiver must have access to the same key. Symmetric encryption is commonly used to encrypt large amounts of data because it is faster and more efficient than asymmetric encryption. However, the main disadvantage of symmetric encryption is that the key must be more carefully secured when it is used

Asymmetric encryption, on the other hand, uses two different keys, a public key and a private key. The public key is used to encrypt the data and the private key is used to decrypt it. The public key can be freely distributed while the private key should only be possessed by a limited number of subjects. Asymmetric encryption is typically used to exchange keys for symmetric encryption and ensure data authenticity.

Due to the fact that encryption requires significant computational resources, the implementation of encryption in big data processing is usually aimed at protecting a narrow area of the total big data set. Owners of big data processing systems (data warehouses, data "lakes") categorize the types of data stored in such systems during partitioning and processing. Data related to personal data, banking, tax, medical, family and other types of secrets stand out among the general array of big data. It is with these categories of data it is reasonable to perform encryption operations, to reduce the computational load on the equipment and more purposeful use of resources. There are both data encryption mechanisms built into the systems of structured database storage and processing and "superimposed" encryption means. An example of a built-in encryption mechanism is the transparent data encryption feature of Oracle database management systems (transparent data encryption).[1] An example of "superimposed" means of encryption of data in a large array is a hardware-software complex Tumar DB, from the Kazakh manufacturer of software and hardware NIL Gamma Technologies LLP. This variant of encryption realizes the requirements for encryption, established in the legislative acts of the Republic of Kazakhstan in accordance with GOST 28147-89 "Information processing systems. Cryptographic protection. Algorithm of cryptographic transformation" and corresponds to the third level of security according to ST RK 1073-2007 "Means of cryptographic protection of information. General technical requirements". Application of this hardware and software method allows to provide encryption of personal data in big data without rewriting the application software that uses this big data array. The data is stored in encrypted form and decrypted on the fly at each request using cryptographic keys stored in a special Hardware security Module (HSM).

In addition to encryption, cryptographic methods for protecting bulk data also include authentication and digital signatures. Authentication is the process of verifying the identity of a user or system. It can be based on the knowledge of a password, the use of biometrics, or the presence of a physical authentication device. Authentication ensures that only authorized users have access to data.

A digital signature, on the other hand, is used to ensure the authenticity and integrity of data. It is a mathematical construct that allows the recipient to verify that the data has not been altered after the signing operation and that it was created by a specific sender. A digital signature is usually created using the sender's private key and can be verified using the sender's public key [15].

Big data also presents unique challenges for cryptographic methods of data protection. One such challenge is the need for high performance when processing and transmitting large amounts of data. Traditional cryptographic algorithms may be too slow to handle such large amounts of data, so specialized algorithms and protocols need to be developed.

Another challenge is the need to ensure data security in distributed big data systems such as cloud computing. In such systems, data may be distributed across multiple nodes, which creates additional vulnerabilities, attack vectors and requires the development of specific defense methods.

Cryptographic methods of large-scale data protection play an important role in ensuring information security in the modern information society. They allow to ensure confidentiality, integrity and authenticity of data, as well as to protect it from unauthorized access and abuse. However, the development and application of effective cryptographic methods for big data is a complex task that requires continuous improvement and development.

2.2 Methods for detecting and preventing attacks on big data storage and processing systems

Methods of ensuring security in big data play an important role in modern information systems. With the emergence of big data and its active use in various fields [16], including banking, there is a need to ensure the security of this information. In this section, we review various methods for ensuring security in big data, as well as methods for detecting and preventing attacks on systems for storing and processing such data.

One of the main methods of providing security in big data is encryption. Encryption protects data from unauthorized access by converting it into a form that is incomprehensible to outsiders. There are different encryption algorithms such as symmetric and asymmetric encryption. Symmetric encryption uses a single key to encrypt and decrypt data, while asymmetric encryption uses a pair of keys - public and private. Encryption allows you to secure data in case of data leakage or unauthorized access.

Another method of providing security in big data is access control. Access control provides the ability to control access to data and resources of the system. There are different access control models such as discretionary access model (DAC), Mandate Access Model (MAC) and Role Based Access Model (RBAC). The DAC model gives the owner of the data the ability to control access to it, the MAC model is based on assigning access levels to objects and subjects, and the RBAC model is based on defining roles and assigning them to users. Access control allows for granularity of access to data and system resources [17].

An additional method of providing security in big data is monitoring and auditing. Monitoring and auditing allow tracking user and system activity, as well as detecting unauthorized actions and attacks on the system. Monitoring and auditing can be implemented using special tools and systems that record and analyze all events that occur in the system. Monitoring and auditing allow timely detection and response to potential security threats in big data.

Another method of providing security in big data is authentication and authorization. Authentication authenticates the user or system and authorization determines the user's access rights to the data and resources of the system. There are various authentication methods such as password authentication, biometric authentication, token-based authentication and others. Authorization is based on defining roles and access rights of users. Authentication and authorization enables security in big data by preventing unauthorized access.

Various methods and technologies are used to detect and prevent attacks on big data storage and processing systems. One such method is machine learning. Machine learning can detect anomalies and unusual patterns in the data, which can indicate the presence of an attack. There are various machine learning algorithms such as classification, clustering and anomaly detection algorithms. Machine learning can create models that can detect attacks on big data storage and processing system.

Another method of detecting and preventing attacks on big data storage and processing systems is network monitoring. Network monitoring allows you to monitor network traffic and detect anomalies that may indicate the presence of an attack. There are various tools and systems for network monitoring such as Intrusion Detection Systems (IDS) and Intrusion Detection and Prevention Systems (IPS). Network monitoring enables timely detection and prevention of attacks on the big data storage and processing system.

An additional method of detecting and preventing attacks on big data storage and processing systems is analyzing event logs. Event logs contain information about user and system activities and possible attacks. Analyzing event logs can identify unusual events and patterns that may indicate the presence of an attack. There are various tools and systems for analyzing event logs, such as event log management systems (SIEM). Analyzing event logs allows you to detect and prevent attacks on big data storage and processing system in a timely manner.

Encryption, access control, monitoring and auditing, authentication and authorization are all methods to ensure security in big data. In addition, methods of attack detection and prevention, such as machine learning, network monitoring and event log analysis, help to detect and prevent attacks on the big data storage and processing system. The development of standards and recommendations on the application of these methods in the banking sector of the Republic of Kazakhstan is an important task to ensure security in big data.

2.3 Data anonymization and pseudonymization techniques in the security context

In this section, we review data anonymization and pseudonymization techniques in the context of security.

Data anonymization is one of the main methods for ensuring security in big data. Its purpose is to remove or replace identifying information such as names, addresses, phone numbers, and other personal information to prevent individuals from being identified. Data anonymization preserves the value of data for analysis and research while ensuring privacy and protecting personal information.

There are several data anonymization techniques that can be applied in the context of big data security. One such method is to replace identifying information with random values. For example, names can be replaced with random alphanumeric characters and addresses can be replaced with random coordinates. This method preserves the structure of the data and provides anonymity, but can make it difficult to analyze and use the data. When using this method, it is important to ensure that identifying information is replaced with the same random values at all data locations. For example, if the implementation of a big data processing system includes a database with several tables, then when anonymizing, the replacement must be done equally in all tables, otherwise the principle of data consistency will be violated and their further analysis and use will be of questionable benefit to companies.

Another method of anonymizing data is generalization. In this method, identifying information is replaced by more generalized values. For example, age can be replaced by categories such as 'young', 'middle-aged' and 'elderly'. This method retains general information about the data but reduces the ability to identify specific individuals.

There is also a method of data anonymization based on encryption. In this method, identifying information is encrypted using special algorithms, and only authorized users have access to the decrypted data. This method provides a high level of security, but makes it difficult to use the data for analysis and research.

Data pseudonymization is another method of providing security in big data. Unlike anonymization, pseudonymization retains the ability to identify individuals, but prevents direct linkage to real identifiers. In pseudonymization, identifying information is replaced with unique identifiers that cannot be directly linked to real data. This allows the data to be used for analysis and research while ensuring privacy and confidentiality.

One of the methods of data pseudonymization is hashing. In this method, identifying information is converted into a unique hash code using special algorithms. The hash code cannot be converted back to the original data, which ensures the security of the identifying information. However, when using hashing it is necessary to take into account the possibility of collisions, when two different data can correspond to the same hash code. An important aspect of using hashing is the choice of a hash sum algorithm that is resistant to tampering at the time of use. For example, the MD5 hashing algorithm, which was widely used earlier, is not considered secure at the moment due to the presence of widely used methods of attacks on it: dictionary brute-force, rainbowcrack, hash collision. Another method of reducing the likelihood of a successful hashing attack is the use of a "salt". A salt is a string of characters that are added to the plaintext and then hashed. "Salting" makes the hashed information more resistant to rainbow table attacks, as this hash variant will have a higher information entropy and therefore less likely to exist in pre-computed rainbow tables.

Another method of data pseudonymization is tokenization. In this method, identifying information is replaced by unique tokens that cannot be directly associated with real data. The tokens can be generated using random values or special algorithms, and only authorized users have the ability to convert the tokens into the corresponding real data.

The use of data anonymization and pseudonymization techniques in banking helps to ensure the confidentiality and protection of customers' personal information when generating large data sets. Data anonymization allows banks to use data for analysis and research, while preventing the possibility of identifying specific customers. Data pseudonymization preserves the ability to identify customers, but prevents direct linkage to real data, ensuring the security of identifying information.

However, it should be kept in mind that no method of anonymizing or pseudonymizing data is completely safe. There are methods and techniques that can be used to de-anonymize or de-pseudonymize data, especially using additional information or statistical methods. Therefore, it is important to take a comprehensive approach to data security, including the use of various anonymization and pseudonymization techniques, encryption, access control and other security measures.

3 ANALYSIS OF EXISTING SECURITY STANDARDS IN THE BANKING SECTOR OF THE REPUBLIC OF KAZAKHSTAN

3.1 Review of current security standards in the banking industry

Banks are key players in the financial system and store a large amount of confidential information about their customers, which makes them particularly attractive to hackers and attackers. Realizing this, the government regulates the banking industry and obliges banks to make efforts and incur financial costs to ensure data security by establishing requirements in laws and regulations, as well as by conducting various types of supervision over the implementation of the established requirements [18].

One of the main documents establishing security requirements for the banks of the Republic of Kazakhstan is "Requirements for ensuring information security of banks, branches of non-resident banks of the Republic of Kazakhstan and organizations engaged in certain types of banking operations" [19]. [19]. These requirements were approved by Resolution No. 48 of the National Bank of the Republic of Kazakhstan dated 27.03.2018 in accordance with the Law of the Republic of Kazakhstan "On Banks and Banking Activities in the Republic of Kazakhstan", and establish requirements for ensuring information security of banks and their infrastructure. The requirements include a number of specific measures, such as protection against unauthorized access, protection against viruses and malware, data encryption, etc. Among the 161 (one hundred and sixty-one) items of the requirements, the following can be highlighted as directly affecting the use of big data in banks:

- responsibility of the first manager of the bank for organization and functioning of the information security management system, as well as the list of functional units and other participants ensuring implementation of information security requirements in the bank;
- the list of confidential information, as well as the procedure for handling protected information, shall be approved by the bank's management body;
- the bank's information security division (hereinafter referred to as IS division) shall ensure detection and analysis of threats, countering attacks and investigation of information security incidents;
- The IS unit defines information security requirements for the use of privileged accounts (e.g., administrative records that have broad authority to access and manage data and the data processing environment;
- the IS division carries out activities to raise awareness of the bank's employees on information security issues;

- the bank's information technology division (hereinafter referred to as the IT division) shall ensure access of employees to information contained in information systems (aspect - confidentiality), as well as configure system and application software with due regard to information security requirements (aspect - integrity and confidentiality) and realize continuous functioning of information systems (aspect - availability);

- the bank's security division implements measures of physical and technical security of equipment processing information, as well as carries out preventive measures aimed at minimizing the risks of information security threats during hiring and dismissal of the bank's employees (insider internal threats);

- the division for work with personnel shall carry out signing by employees of the bank, as well as persons engaged to work under the agreement on rendering services, trainees, interns, trainees of obligations on non-disclosure of confidential information;

- banks shall appoint owners for information systems containing confidential data who are responsible for compliance with information security requirements when creating, implementing, modifying, operating information systems and providing products and services to customers and subdivisions of the bank, as well as when integrating information systems with external information systems;

The Bank categorizes information assets processing confidential data by dividing them into critical and non-critical ones based on the level of losses from violation of their confidentiality, integrity, availability;

- the Bank shall ensure application of anti-virus protection means on the infrastructure elements processing confidential data;

- the bank shall keep records in the form of a list of all software, as well as all cryptographic means of information protection, which are allowed before processing confidential information;

- the bank shall ensure audit trail of operations of access to confidential data;

- the bank implements the necessary complexity of passwords used when accessing sensitive data;

- the bank shall ensure implementation of organizational and software and hardware measures limiting the possibility of unauthorized copying of data to removable data carriers;

- The bank forms a network perimeter limiting the possibility of unauthorized network connections to arrays of confidential data;

- The bank provides realization of isolated from each other industrial and test environments, as well as development environment when working with big data;

- When confidential information is used in testing and development environments, the necessary protection measures are applied to these environments;

- the bank shall ensure timely installation of security updates in information systems;

- the bank shall scan information systems processing confidential information for vulnerabilities and shall ensure elimination of identified vulnerabilities.

In addition to the "48 Requirements", for banks, information security requirements with varying levels of detail are specified in the twenty-six (26) by-laws listed in Table 1 to this paper.

Another important standard is the Payment Card Industry Data Security Standard (PCI DSS). This standard was developed by the international community of payment systems and establishes requirements for the security of data related to payment cards. According to this standard, banks must ensure the protection of payment card holders' data, as well as ensure the security of the processes of processing and transmission of this data. A distinctive feature of the requirements of this standard is a direct prohibition to store the most sensitive data (full card numbers, CVV codes, PIN codes of payment cards) in open (unencrypted) form.

In addition, banks need to comply with the requirements of the legislation of the Republic of Kazakhstan in the field of personal data protection. In accordance with the law "On Personal Data and their Protection", banks are obliged to ensure confidentiality and protection of their customers' personal data. For this purpose, they need to apply modern methods of data encryption, control access to personal data and ensure its safety and integrity. One of the legal requirements limiting the use of big data by banks is the requirement to locate personal data on the territory of the Republic of Kazakhstan (paragraph 2, Article 12, paragraph 2 of the Law of the Republic of Kazakhstan "On personal data and their protection").

Another important standard is ISO/IEC 27001, which defines the requirements for an information security management system. It sets requirements for risk management process, security policy, asset management and many other aspects of information security. ISO/IEC 27001 is an international standard and can be used in the banking sector to ensure data security [21], while it is important to understand that the use of this standard is not mandatory for banks in Kazakhstan.

There are also guidelines developed by various organizations and associations that deal with data security in banking. One such organization is the National Institute of Standards and Technology (NIST), which has developed a number of recommendations and guidelines on data security. For example, NIST SP 800-53 defines a set of security controls that should be implemented to ensure information security in information systems [22].

It is also worth noting the recommendations and standards developed by international banking associations such as SWIFT and the International Organization of Securities Commissions (IOSCO). SWIFT approved Swift Customer Security control Framework [23], which defines the requirements for data security in interbank payment systems, including authentication, encryption and access control. IOSCO develops standards and recommendations to ensure data security in the field of securities and financial markets.

The analysis of existing standards and recommendations allows us to identify several basic principles and approaches that can be applied in the development of practical standards and recommendations on data security in the banking sector of the Republic of Kazakhstan.

First, it is important to consider data protection principles at all stages of the data lifecycle - from collection and storage to transmission and deletion. This includes regular security updates, monitoring and analyzing activity, encrypting data during storage and transmission, and properly managing access to data.

Second, it is necessary to ensure data protection at the physical and logical levels. Physical protection includes the use of secure premises for storing servers and equipment, controlling access to confidential information processing rooms, use of video surveillance, physical security and other security measures. Logical protection includes data encryption, user authentication, access control and multi-level protection of information systems, network shielding of systems, protection of attack systems, monitoring of event logs, control of privileged users' actions, timely data backup.

Thirdly, it is important to take into account the specifics of the banking industry and the requirements of regulators. The banking industry is characterized by a high degree of regulation and requires compliance with certain data security standards [24]. Regulators can set requirements for data encryption, access control, backup and other security aspects.

Fourth, it is important to consider the threats and risks associated with the use of big data. Big data represents a huge amount of information that can be used by attackers to obtain sensitive data. Therefore, it is necessary to apply protection measures such as monitoring network activity, anomaly detection and data leakage prevention. Requirements for information security risk management in the Republic of Kazakhstan are approved by the Resolution of the Management Board of the Agency of the Republic of Kazakhstan on Regulation and Development of Financial Market No. 111 dated November 23, 2020. "On approval of the information security risk assessment methodology, including the procedure for ranking financial organizations by the degree of exposure to information security risks", as well as in the Resolution of the Management Board of the Agency of the Republic of Kazakhstan on

Regulation and Development of Financial Market No. 188 dated 12.11.2019. "On Approval of the Rules for Formation of Risk Management and Internal Control System for Second-tier Banks".

Fifth, it is important to consider international standards and guidelines, as many banks have international operations and work with customers from different countries. When developing practical standards and guidelines, the requirements of PCI DSS, ISO/IEC 27001, NIST SP 800-53, GDPR (General Data Protection Regulation) and other international standards should be taken into account.

3.2 Assessing the effectiveness of existing standards in the banking sector of the Republic of Kazakhstan

The Republic of Kazakhstan is actively developing its banking sector and strives to ensure a high level of data security. Currently, there are enough standards and guiding documents, security regulations in the country that regulate the activities of banks and ensure the protection of information. The main document is the "Requirements for ensuring information security of banks, branches of non-resident banks of the Republic of Kazakhstan and organizations engaged in certain types of banking operations" mentioned in the previous section, approved by the Resolution of the Board of the ARRFR No. 48 dated 27.03.2018 (hereinafter - IS Requirements for BVU). This document establishes the requirements for information protection, as well as determines the procedures and security measures to be taken by banks.

In order to assess the effectiveness of application of existing security regulations in the banking sector of the Republic of Kazakhstan, it is necessary to consider several aspects. First, it is necessary to analyze their compliance with international norms and recommendations in the field of information security, because the banking sector is a part of the global economy, and its security should be relevant to international threats and security requirements.

Secondly, it is necessary to assess the effectiveness of application of regulatory documents in the practice of the banking sector of the Republic of Kazakhstan. For this purpose, it is possible to analyze cases of data security breaches and assess how successfully standards and other documents were applied to prevent such incidents. Such analysis will allow to identify problem areas and offer recommendations for their improvement.

The third aspect that should be considered when assessing the effectiveness of existing security standards is the degree of awareness and training of banking personnel. Data security depends not only on technical security measures, but primarily on the knowledge and skills of employees. Therefore, it is important to assess the effectiveness of staff education and training in the field of information security.

In addition, it is worth considering the degree of customer satisfaction in the banking sector in the Republic of Kazakhstan. If customers feel that their data are reliably protected and information security is a priority for banks, this indicates that the application of existing security standards is highly effective.

In general, the effectiveness of existing security standards in the banking sector of the Republic of Kazakhstan can be assessed by several criteria: compliance with international requirements, success in preventing security incidents, staff training and customer satisfaction. Such an analysis will allow to identify problem areas and develop recommendations for improving security standards in the banking sector of the Republic of Kazakhstan.

If we consider the first aspect concerning the comparison of international experience and legislative requirements for information security of Kazakhstan, then when analyzing the compliance of the norms of the IS Requirements for TLDs [25] and the internationally recognized methodology (Center of Internet Security) CIS Critical Security Controls v8, it can be seen that the coverage of the regulatory act of Kazakhstan provides 94 (ninety-four) % of CIS Critical Security Controls [26] (for level 1). At the same time, the remaining uncovered positions (6 (six) %) are fully reflected in another regulatory act of the Republic of Kazakhstan, which has a narrower scope (Resolution of the Board of the ARFMR No. 90 dated September 21, 2020. "On Approval of Requirements for Information Security Incident Response Services, Internal Investigations of Information Security Incidents"). A more detailed analysis of the coverage of information security requirements in the documents is given in Table 1.

Thus, the current information security regulation of the banking industry is fully compliant in its basic version with international regulatory experience.

Table 1 - CIS Critical Security Controls requirement (level 1)

Name	Coverage of IS Requirements for Tier 2 Banks (48th IS Requirements)
1. inventory and control of enterprise assets Actively manage (inventory, track, and correct) all enterprise assets (end-user devices, including handheld and mobile; network devices; non-computer/Internet of Things (IoT) devices; servers) connected to the infrastructure physically, virtually, remotely, and in the cloud to know exactly all assets that need to be controlled and protected in the enterprise. This will also help identify unauthorized and unmanaged assets for removal or remediation.	
1.1 Create and maintain a detailed inventory of equipment (device) assets. Create and maintain an accurate, detailed and up-to-date inventory of all enterprise assets capable of storing or processing data, including: end-user devices (including handheld and mobile), network devices , and non-computing/IoT devices and servers. Ensure that the inventory records the network address (if static), hardware address, machine name, data asset owner, department for each asset, and whether the asset has been approved for network connectivity. For mobile end-user devices, this process can be supported by tools like MDM if needed. This inventory includes assets connected to the infrastructure physically, virtually, remotely, and assets in the cloud. It also includes assets that regularly connect to the enterprise network infrastructure, even if they are not under the control of the enterprise. Review and update the inventory of all enterprise assets twice a year or more frequently.	25,66
1.2 Remediating unauthorized assets Ensure that there is a process in place to remediate unauthorized assets on a weekly basis. The enterprise may choose to remove the asset from the network, prevent it from remotely connecting to the network, or quarantine the asset.	83,84
2- Inventory and control software assets Actively manage (inventory, monitor, and remediate) all software (operating systems and applications) on the network so that only authorized software is installed and executed, and unauthorized and unmanaged software is detected and prevented from being installed or executed.	

2.1 Create and maintain a software inventory Create and maintain a detailed inventory of all licensed software installed on enterprise assets. The software inventory should include the name, manufacturer, date of initial installation/use, and business purpose for each entry; if applicable, include the Uniform Resource Locator (URL), application store(s), version(s), deployment mechanism, and decommissioning date. Review and update the software registry twice a year or more frequently.	43,52,79,102
2.2 Ensure that authorized software is currently supported Ensure that the software inventory for enterprise assets lists only currently supported software as authorized. If the software is not supported but is necessary to accomplish the enterprise mission, document the exception, detailing mitigating controls and compensating risk acceptance. Designate any unsupported software that does not have exception documentation as unauthorized. Review the software list to verify software support at least monthly or more frequently.	43,52,79,102
2.3 Remediation of unauthorized software Ensure that unauthorized software is either removed from use on enterprise assets or receives a documented exception. Verify monthly or more frequently.	43,52,79,102
3. Data Protection Develop processes and technical controls to identify, classify, securely process, store and dispose of data.	
3.1 Establish and maintain a data governance process Establish and maintain a data governance process. This process should address data sensitivity, data owner, data handling, data retention limits, and data deletion requirements based on the sensitivity and data retention standards for the enterprise. Review and update documentation annually, or when significant changes occur in the enterprise that may affect this Security.	98,103
3.2 Create and maintain a data inventory Create and maintain a data inventory based on the enterprise data management process. Inventory sensitive data, at a minimum. Review and update inventory annually, at a minimum, prioritizing sensitive data.	98,103
3.3 Customizing Data Access Control Lists Customize data access control lists based on user knowledge needs. Apply data access control lists, also known as access permissions, to local and remote file systems, databases, and applications.	37,65
3.4 Ensure data retention Retain data in accordance with the enterprise data management process. Data retention should include minimum and maximum retention periods.	98,111,114

3.5 Safely dispose of data Safely dispose of data in accordance with the enterprise data management process. Ensure that the disposal process and method is commensurate with the sensitivity of the data.	43,79,143
3.6 Encrypting data on end-user devices Encrypting data on end-user devices containing sensitive data. Example implementations may include: Windows BitLocker®, Apple FileVault®, Linux® dm-crypt.	43,79,143
4. Secure Configuration of Enterprise Assets and Software Create and maintain a secure configuration of enterprise assets (end-user devices, including portable and mobile; network devices; non-computing/IoT devices; and servers) and software (operating systems and applications).	
4.1 Establish and Maintain a Secure Configuration Process Establish and maintain a secure configuration process for enterprise assets (end-user devices, including portable and mobile; non-computer/IoT devices; and servers) and software (operating systems and applications). Review and update documentation annually or when significant changes occur in the enterprise that may affect this Security.	137,44,96,43,79,90
4.2 Establish and maintain a secure configuration process for network infrastructure Establish and maintain a secure configuration process for network devices. Review and update documentation annually, or when significant changes occur in the enterprise that may affect this Security.	96,43,79,85,90
4.3 Configuring Automatic Session Lockout on Enterprise Assets Configure automatic session lockout on enterprise assets after a specified period of inactivity. For general-purpose operating systems, this period should not exceed 15 minutes. For end-user mobile devices, this period should not exceed 2 minutes.	43,79
4.4 Implement and manage a firewall on servers Implement and manage a firewall on servers, if supported. Examples of implementations include a virtual firewall, an operating system firewall, or a third-party firewall agent.	43,79,83,84
4.5 Implement and manage a firewall on end-user devices Implement and manage a host-based firewall or port filtering tool on end-user devices, with a default deny rule that discards all traffic except those services and ports that are explicitly allowed.	43,79,83,84
4.6 Secure Enterprise Asset and Software Management Securely manage enterprise assets and software. Examples of implementations include configuration management using infrastructure as version-controlled code and access to administrative interfaces over secure network protocols such as Secure Shell (SSH) and Hypertext Transfer	137,44

Protocol Secure (HTTPS). Do not use insecure management protocols such as Telnet (teletype network) and HTTP unless necessary for operations.	
4.7 Managing default accounts on enterprise assets and software Manage default accounts on enterprise assets and software, such as root, administrator, and other pre-configured vendor accounts. Example implementations may include: disabling default accounts or rendering them unusable.	41,65,101,137,43,79
5. Account Management Use processes and tools to assign and manage credential authorization for user accounts, including administrator accounts, as well as service, enterprise asset, and software accounts.	
5.1 Create and maintain an inventory of accounts Use unique passwords for all enterprise assets. Implementation best practices include, at a minimum, an 8-character password for accounts using MFA and a 14-character password for accounts not using MFA.	67,68,101,137,99,43,79
5.2 Use unique passwords Use unique passwords for all corporate assets. Best practice includes at least an 8-character password for accounts that use MFA and a 14-character password for accounts that do not use MFA.	39,40,48,71,72
5.3 Disabling Inactive Accounts Delete or disable inactive accounts after 45 days of inactivity, if supported.	67,68,101
5.4 Limit administrator privileges to dedicated administrator accounts Limit administrator privileges to dedicated administrator accounts on enterprise assets. Perform common computing activities, such as browsing the Internet, e-mail, and using the productivity suite, from a primary, unprivileged user account.	67,68,65,101,99,43,79
6. Access Control Management Use processes and tools to create, assign, manage, and revoke access credentials and privileges for user, administrator, and service accounts for enterprise assets and software.	
6.1 Establish a process for granting access Establish and follow a process, preferably automated, for granting access to enterprise assets when a user is newly hired, granted rights, or changes role.	67,68,65,101,99,43,79

6.2 Establish a process for revoking access Establish and follow a process, preferably automated, for revoking access to enterprise assets by disabling accounts immediately upon termination of employment, revocation of rights, or change of user role. Disabling accounts rather than deleting them may be necessary to preserve audit records.	67,68,65,101,99,43,79
6.3 Require MFA for externally accessible applications Require that all enterprise or third-party externally accessible applications provide MFA, if supported. Providing MFA through a directory service or SSO vendor is a satisfactory implementation of this assurance.	39,40,48,71,72,86,74,87
6.4 Require MFA for remote network access Require MFA for remote network access.	39,40,48,71,72,86
6.5 Require MFA for administrative access Require MFA for all administrative access accounts, where supported, on all enterprise assets, whether managed independently or through a third-party vendor.	39,40,48,71,72
7. Continuous Vulnerability Management Develop a plan to continuously assess and track vulnerabilities across all enterprise assets in your infrastructure to eliminate and minimize opportunities for attackers. Track information about new threats and vulnerabilities from public and private sources.	
7.1 Establish and maintain a vulnerability management process Establish and maintain a documented vulnerability management process for enterprise assets. Review and update documentation annually or when significant changes occur in the enterprise that may affect this Security.	102,120,122,124,125,99,43,79,85,49,115,119
7.2 Establish and maintain a remediation process Establish and maintain a risk-based remediation strategy documented in the remediation process, with monthly or more frequent reviews.	102,120,122,124,125,99,43,79,85,49,115,119
7.3 Perform automated operating system patch management Perform operating system upgrades on enterprise assets using automated patch management on a monthly or more frequent basis.	102,120,122,124,125,99,43,79,49,115,119
7.4 Perform automated application patch management Perform application updates on enterprise assets using automated patch management on a monthly or more frequent basis.	102,120,122,124,125,99,43,79,49,115,119
8. Audit Log Management Collect, alert, view, and store audit logs of events that can help detect, understand, or recover from an attack.	
8.1 Establish and maintain an audit log management process Establish and maintain an audit log management process that defines the enterprise's logging requirements. At a minimum, this addresses the collection, review, and retention of audit logs for enterprise assets. Review and update documentation annually or	59,65,101,44,111,114,14,83,84

when significant changes occur in the enterprise that may affect this Security.	
8.2 Collect audit logs Collect audit logs. Ensure that logging in accordance with the enterprise's audit log management process has been enabled for all enterprise assets.	59,65,101,44,111,114,14,83,84,43,79
8.3 Ensure adequate storage of audit logs Ensure that logging locations maintain sufficient storage to comply with the enterprise audit log management process.	59,65,101,44,111,114,14
8. Protect email and web browsers Improve protection and detection of threats originating from email and web browsers, as this gives attackers the opportunity to manipulate people's behavior by directly interacting with them.	
9.1 Ensure that only fully supported browsers and email clients are used Ensure that only fully supported browsers and email clients are allowed in the enterprise, using only the latest versions of browsers and email clients provided by the vendor.	102,120,122,124,125,43,79,49,115,119
9.2 Use DNS Filtering Services Use DNS filtering services on all corporate resources to block access to known malicious domains.	74,87,49,115,119
10. Malware Protection Prevent or control the installation, distribution, and execution of malicious applications, code, or scripts on corporate assets.	
10.1 Deploy and maintain anti-virus software Deploy and maintain anti-virus software on all enterprise assets.	43,79,49,115,119
10.2 Configuring Automatic Updates of Anti-Virus Program Signatures Configure automatic updates of anti-virus program signature files on all enterprise assets.	43,79,49,115,119
10.3 Disabling autorun and autoplay for removable media Disable the auto start and auto playback functions for removable media.	43,79,49,115,119,75
11. Data Recovery Develop and maintain data recovery methods sufficient to return enterprise assets to a pre-incident and trusted state.	
11.1 Establish and maintain a data recovery process Establish and maintain a data recovery process. This process should address data recovery scope of work, recovery priorities, and security of backup data. Review and update documentation annually or when significant changes occur in the enterprise that may affect this Security.	48,83,84

11.2 Performing automatic backups Perform automatic backups of enterprise assets. Perform backups weekly or more frequently, depending on the sensitivity of the data.	48,83,84,43,79, 75
11.3 Protecting recovery data Protect recovery data with controls equivalent to the original data. Encrypt or segregate data as required.	48,83,84
11.4 Create and maintain an isolated instance of recovery data Create and maintain an isolated instance of recovery data. Example implementations include version control of backups through offline, cloud, or offsite systems or services.	48,83,84
12. Network Infrastructure Create, implement, and actively manage (monitor, report, remediate) network devices to prevent attackers from exploiting vulnerable network services and access points.	
12.1 Ensure that the network infrastructure is kept up to date Ensure that the network infrastructure is kept up to date. Examples of implementation include using the latest stable software release and/or using currently supported Network as a Service (NaaS) offerings. Check software versions monthly or more frequently to ensure software is supported.	102,120,122,43, 79,85
14. Security Awareness and Skills Training Establish and maintain a security awareness program to influence employee behavior so that they are security aware and have the necessary skills to mitigate enterprise cybersecurity risks.	
14.1 Establish and maintain a security awareness program Establish and maintain a security awareness program. The purpose of a security awareness program is to educate enterprise employees on how to interact safely with enterprise assets and data. Provide training upon hire and at least annually. Review and update the content annually, or when significant changes occur in the enterprise that may affect this security program.	143,107,108,49, 115,119
14.2 Train employees to recognize social engineering attacks Train employees to recognize social engineering attacks such as phishing, pre-messaging, and tracking searches	107,108,49,115, 119
14.3 Train employees on authentication best practices. Train employees on authentication best practices. Example topics include MFA, password composition, and credential management.	107,108
14.4 Train employees on best practices for handling data. Train employees on how to identify and properly store, transfer, archive, and destroy sensitive data. This also includes training employees on clean screen and desktop best practices, such as locking the screen when they step away from their corporate	143,98,49,115,1 19

resource, erasing physical and virtual whiteboards at the end of meetings, and securely storing data and assets	
14.5 Educate employees about the causes of unintentional accidents Train employees to be aware of the causes of unintentional data disclosure. Examples include improper delivery of sensitive data, loss of an end user's handheld device, or release of data to an undesirable audience.	107,108
14.6 Employee Recognition and Reporting Training Train employees to recognize and be able to report a potential incident.	107,108,49,115, 119
14.7 Train employees on how to identify and report if their corporate assets are not receiving security updates. Train employees on how to check for and report outdated software patches or any failures in automated processes and tools. Part of this training should include notifying IT staff of any failures in automated processes and tools.	107,108,49,115, 119
14.8 Train employees on the dangers of connecting to and transmitting corporate data over insecure networks Train employees on the dangers of connecting to and transmitting data over insecure networks within the enterprise. If the enterprise has remote employees, training should include guidance on how to ensure that the home network infrastructure is set up securely for all users.	107,108
15. Service Provider Management Develop a process to evaluate service providers that store sensitive data or are responsible for critical enterprise IT platforms or processes to ensure that these providers are protecting these platforms and data appropriately.	
15.1 Establish and maintain a roster of service providers Establish and maintain a roster of service providers. The roster should list all known service providers, indicate classification, and assign an enterprise contact for each service provider. Review and update the list annually or when significant changes occur in the enterprise that may affect security.	59,103
17. Incident Response Management Establish a program to develop and maintain incident response capabilities (e.g., policies, plans, procedures, defined roles, training, and communications) to prepare for, detect, and rapidly respond to attacks.	

17.1 Designate personnel to manage incident handling Designate one key person and at least one backup person to manage incident handling within the enterprise. The managing staff is responsible for coordinating and documenting incident response and recovery efforts and may consist of staff within the enterprise, third-party vendors, or a hybrid approach. If a third-party vendor is used, designate at least one staff member within the enterprise to oversee the third-party vendor. Review annually or when significant changes occur in the enterprise that may affect this Safety.	
17.2 Establish and maintain contact information for reporting Security Incidents. Establish and maintain contact information for parties who need to be informed of security incidents. Contacts may include internal personnel, third-party vendors, law enforcement, cyber insurance providers, relevant government agencies. Agencies, Information Sharing and Analysis Center (ISAC) partners, or other stakeholders. Review contacts annually to ensure information is up to date.	
17.3 Establish and maintain an organization-wide process for reporting incidents. Establish and maintain an organization-wide process for employees to report security incidents. The process includes reporting deadlines, personnel to report, reporting mechanism, and minimum information to be reported. Make the process publicly available to all employees. Review annually or when there are significant changes to the enterprise that may affect this Security.	

Regarding the second aspect related to the assessment of the effectiveness of application of regulatory documents in the practice of the banking sector of the Republic of Kazakhstan through the analysis of cases of data security breaches, the rather closed type of information on information security incidents in banks significantly complicates such analysis. The following data available in open sources on IS incidents in banks can be noted:

- The banking sector regulator points to 64 cyber incidents in Kazakhstan's financial organizations in 2023;
- Data leakage of 12 million Kazpost customer records [27];
- Funds were stolen from 500 bank cards through the Woopay.kz payment system [28];
- Phishing attack on behalf of a Jusan Bank employee [29];
- Embezzlement of 2 billion tenge from two banks in Kazakhstan in 2016-2017 [30];
- Failure in the payment system of SB "Alfa Bank" JSC with unauthorized transfers in the amount of 416 million tg[31];

- Statistics of the State Technical Service under the KNB RK for the first half of 2021 [32];

Thus, the lack of complete and open information for the last 5 years and the fragmentation of information available in the media does not allow us to draw conclusions about the level of efficiency of regulation of the banking industry. There is a gradual increase in the regulatory impact on financial market participants, which is due to the development of the function and increase in the resources spent by the state in this area (the specialized regulator in March 2023 expanded the number of specialists in the area of regulation of information security requirements and created the Department of Information and Cybersecurity) [33].

Regarding the third aspect related to the assessment of the effectiveness of the application of existing security standards through the level of awareness and training of personnel in the banking sector, it can be noted that in 2020 the specialized regulator approved a bylaw obliging the second-tier banks of Kazakhstan to conduct annual training and have heads of information security departments certified according to international certifications[34].

At the same time, this regulation has been finalized several times and the requirements have been strengthened in 2021 and 2022 [35].

4 DEVELOPMENT OF STANDARDS AND GUIDELINES FOR SECURITY IN BIG DATA

4.1 Analyzing Big Data Security Challenges and Vulnerabilities in the Banking Industry

The development of standards and recommendations for security in big data is an important task in today's information society. Big Data, or Big Data, are huge amounts of information that are processed and stored using various technologies and algorithms [36]. The banking industry is one of the areas where big data security is of particular importance as it is related to processing and storing sensitive financial information of customers.

The analysis of problems and vulnerabilities in the field of big data security in the banking industry allows us to identify the main threats and risks that may arise when processing and storing large amounts of data [37]. One of the main problems is unauthorized access to data. Database hacking and information leakage can lead to serious financial losses and damage to the bank's reputation. In addition, big data may contain personal information of customers, which should be protected in accordance with the requirements of the legislation on personal data protection.

One of the vulnerabilities in big data security is inadequate protection of the network infrastructure. A bank's network can be vulnerable to hackers trying to access data or disrupt system operations. Inadequate network protection can lead to information leakage or disruption of banking operations. It is important to note that the existing regulatory requirements for second-tier banks in Kazakhstan prescribe mandatory firewalling of information infrastructure processing confidential information, as well as separation of test and production data processing environments.

The list of the most common vulnerabilities of information technologies that process big data can be investigated using the OWASP Data Security Top 10 [38] prepared by the Open Worldwide Application Security Project (OWASP), an open source application security project.

According to the OWASP Data Security Top 10, the following types of vulnerabilities are the most common and their remediation methods are summarized in Table 2.

Table 2 - Most common vulnerabilities and remediation methods according to OWASP Data Security Top 10

Name of attack	Attack Description	Recommendations on methods to mitigate the risk of a successful attack

Data injection	unauthorized individuals exploit vulnerabilities to inject malicious code or commands that could compromise data integrity and confidentiality)	1. Use parameterized queries or prepared instructions to prevent SQL injection. 2. Implement input validation and clean user input to block malware injection. 3. Use web application firewalls (WAFs) to detect and block injection attacks.
Authentication and access control violation	Weak authentication mechanisms, incomplete access control or improperly configured permissions that allow unauthorized access to sensitive data	1. Enforce strong password policies, including password complexity requirements and regular password updates. 2. Implement multi-factor authentication (MFA) to add an extra layer of security. 3. Apply the principle of least privilege, ensuring that users only have access to the resources they need.
Data leaks	Unauthorized disclosure or theft of sensitive data, jeopardizing its confidentiality and potentially leading to legal and reputational consequences	1. Regularly patch and update software and systems to address vulnerabilities. 2. Implement intrusion detection and prevention systems (IDPS) to detect and block unauthorized access attempts. 3. Encrypt sensitive data both in storage and in transmission to protect it from unauthorized access.
Malware and ransomware attacks	Infection with malicious software that can jeopardize data availability, confidentiality and integrity, often through phishing attacks or vulnerabilities in software that has not been updated.	1. Implement robust anti-virus and anti-malware solutions and keep them up to date. 2. Regularly train employees on safe browsing practices and the dangers of opening suspicious attachments or visiting untrusted websites. 3. Keep up-to-date backups of your critical data to mitigate ransomware attacks.
Threats from insiders	Malicious or unintentional actions by authorized users, such as employees or contractors, that result in unauthorized access, misuse or	1. Implement robust access controls, ensuring that employees only have access to the data and systems necessary for their job functions. 2. Track and log user activity to detect suspicious behavior or data theft. 3. Conduct regular security training to inform employees about security policies and the risks associated with unauthorized data processing.

	disclosure of sensitive data	
Insufficient cryptographic support	Inadequate encryption practices, including weak algorithms, improper key management, or lack of encryption, making data vulnerable to unauthorized access or tampering	1. Use strong and up-to-date encryption algorithms and protocols. 2. Implement appropriate key management practices, including secure storage, rotation, and distribution of encryption keys. 3. Regularly test and update encryption mechanisms in accordance with industry best practices.
Insecure data processing	Improper storage, transfer or disposal of sensitive data leading to accidental disclosure or loss	1. Implement strong access controls and encryption mechanisms to protect data in storage and transmission. 2. Regularly evaluate and update data handling procedures in accordance with industry standards and regulations. 3. Implement secure data disposal methods, including securely deleting or destroying data when it is no longer needed.
Insufficient security from third parties	Inadequate security measures by third-party vendors or integrations that create vulnerabilities that can be exploited for unauthorized access to data	1. Conduct a thorough security assessment of third-party vendors before entering into a business partnership. 2. Implement a vendor risk management program to evaluate and monitor third-party security practices. 3. Regularly review and update contracts and agreements, including security requirements and expectations.
Poor data inventory and data management	An incomplete or inaccurate inventory of digital assets and insufficient data management practices, leading to difficulties in protecting and securing data	1. Conduct regular asset discovery and inventory management to identify and catalog all digital assets. 2. Implement a data classification structure to categorize data based on confidentiality and apply appropriate security measures accordingly. 3. Establish data management policies and procedures, including data storage, access controls, and secure deletion methods.
Non-compliance with data	Failure to comply with applicable data protection, industry standards	1. Study the relevant data protection regulations and standards applicable to your organization's operations and the data you process.

protection requirements	and legal requirements, exposing organizations to legal risks and reputational damage	2. Conduct a thorough assessment of your data processing activities to identify any compliance gaps. 3. Develop and implement robust data protection policies, procedures and controls to ensure compliance with applicable regulations. 4. Regularly review and update your data protection practices as regulations evolve and new requirements emerge. 5. Provide employees with training and awareness programs to ensure they understand their responsibilities and the importance of compliance. 6. Conduct periodic audits and assessments to monitor compliance and identify areas for improvement. 7. Engage legal counsel or data protection experts to ensure compliance with legal requirements and best practices. 8. Maintain appropriate documentation and records to demonstrate compliance efforts.

In order to address the challenges and vulnerabilities of big data security in the banking industry, it is necessary to develop customized protective measures that are economically justified in each specific application. Existing international guidelines should be utilized to ensure robust data protection.

One of the main aspects of a set of requirements for big data protection should be data privacy. Data privacy is important to protect customers' personal data, bank secrets and commercial information. This requires the use of modern encryption algorithms and access control mechanisms that will restrict access to data to only authorized persons.

Data integrity is also an important aspect. Data integrity ensures that information has not been altered or corrupted inappropriately. This requires the use of integrity control mechanisms that will detect any alteration or substitution of data. In addition, data backup mechanisms should be developed to allow data to be restored in the event of loss or damage, thus ensuring the necessary level of data availability (i.e., the ability to retrieve and use information at the right time).

In order to secure the network infrastructure, standards and guidelines need to be developed to protect the network from external attacks. This may include the use of advanced defenses such as firewalls, intrusion detection systems and monitoring systems. In addition, regular network security audits and testing should be conducted to identify and remediate vulnerabilities.

Another important aspect of security in big data is security monitoring and analysis. Monitoring allows you to track user activity, detect anomalous behavior, and prevent security incidents. Security analysis allows identifying vulnerabilities and weaknesses in the system, and provides information for making decisions to improve security. To ensure security in the banking sector of the Republic of Kazakhstan, it is recommended to use a comprehensive approach that includes various methods and technologies. Important components of such an approach are data encryption, user authentication and authorization, security monitoring and analysis, and employee training and awareness.

For banks that are issuers of payment cards, one of the main security standards in the banking industry is PCI DSS (Payment Card Industry Data Security Standard). This standard establishes requirements for payment card data security and includes measures such as network protection, data encryption, access restriction, etc. Implementation and compliance with PCI DSS is mandatory. Implementation and compliance with PCI DSS is mandatory for all banks accepting payment card payments.

In addition, other standards and guidelines such as ISO/IEC 27001, ITIL, COBIT and others can be applied to ensure security in the banking industry. These standards provide guidance on information security management, including the establishment of policies, procedures and controls.

In conclusion, providing security in big data is a challenging and important task in today's information society. For this purpose it is necessary to apply various methods and technologies, such as data encryption, user authentication and authorization, security monitoring and analysis. In the banking sector of the Republic of Kazakhstan it is especially important to ensure security in big data because of the large volume of sensitive information and various threats. For this purpose, it is recommended to apply a comprehensive approach including various standards and recommendations such as PCI DSS, ISO/IEC 27001, ITIL, COBIT and others.

4.2 Development of new standards and guidelines for security in big data in banking industry

The development of standards and recommendations to ensure security in big data is an urgent task in today's information society. Big Data, or Big Data, are voluminous and complex data sets that require special methods and tools for their processing, storage and analysis.

However, with the increase of data volumes in the financial sector the problem of their security arises, as big data contains a lot of confidential and sensitive information, and there are quite different places of data storage: file containers on workstations and servers, relational and non-relational databases placed on the server infrastructure of companies and third parties (cloud data processing), various cloud applications used under the SaaS (Software as a Service) model, corporate data warehouses, data storage, data storage, etc. Each place of data storage is characterized by the following features: file containers on workstations and servers, relational and non-relational databases placed on the server infrastructure of companies and third parties (cloud data processing), various cloud applications used under the SaaS (Software as a Service) model, corporate data warehouses, data storage, data storage, etc. Each data storage location is characterized by a unique set of threats that can put data confidentiality, availability and integrity at risk.

In the banking industry, the processing of big data is particularly important because banks contain a large amount of personal customer data as well as financial information, and because of the ever-changing landscape of the banks' infrastructure, continuously following the latest trends in information processing technologies. Therefore, the development of new standards and guidelines to ensure security in big data in banking is a necessity.

One of the main aspects of security in big data is to protect data from unauthorized access. To do this, various methods of user authentication and authorization as well as data encryption must be used. For example, two-factor authentication can be used where the user has to provide two different factors to prove their identity such as password and fingerprint. It is also necessary to encrypt data, both while it is being stored and while it is being transmitted over the network.

Another important aspect of security in big data is the detection and prevention of attacks on the data processing system. This requires the use of specialized data monitoring and analysis systems that can detect abnormal user behavior or unusual database queries. It is also necessary to regularly update software and apply security patches to protect the system from known vulnerabilities.

Another important aspect of security in big data is data integrity. Data integrity means that the data has not been altered or tampered with without authorization. Various techniques such as data hashing and checksums can be used to ensure data integrity. Data hashing allows you to create a unique identifier for each block of data that will change if the data changes. Checksums allow checking the integrity of the data by comparing the checksum of the received data with the expected checksum. This approach is widely used in automatic mode in distributed storage registry technologies.

In addition, an important aspect of security in big data is data privacy. Data confidentiality means that only authorized users have access to the data and other individuals cannot access the data. Encryption techniques such as symmetric and asymmetric encryption can be used to ensure data confidentiality. Symmetric encryption uses the same key to encrypt and decrypt data, while asymmetric encryption uses different keys to encrypt and decrypt data.

After reviewing the concept of Big Data, existing data protection methods and standards, we can conclude that Big Data security methods can be grouped into four areas, such as infrastructure security (e.g., secure distributed computing using MapReduce), data confidentiality (e.g., data mining that preserves confidentiality/detailed access), data governance (e.g., secure data provenance and storage), and integrity and reactive security (e.g., data integrity and reactive security).

Each of these aspects faces the following security challenges:

1. Infrastructure security
2. Data privacy
   - Intelligent data analysis with privacy-preserving analytics.
   - Cryptographic solutions for data security
   - Access control
3. Data management and integrity
   - Secure storage of data and transaction logs
   - Detailed audit
   - Data origin
4. Reactive safety
5. End-to-end filtering and verification
6. Real-time monitoring of the security level.

These security and privacy concerns span the entire spectrum of the big data lifecycle (Figure 1): data production sources (devices), the data itself, data processing, data storage, data transportation, and data use across devices.

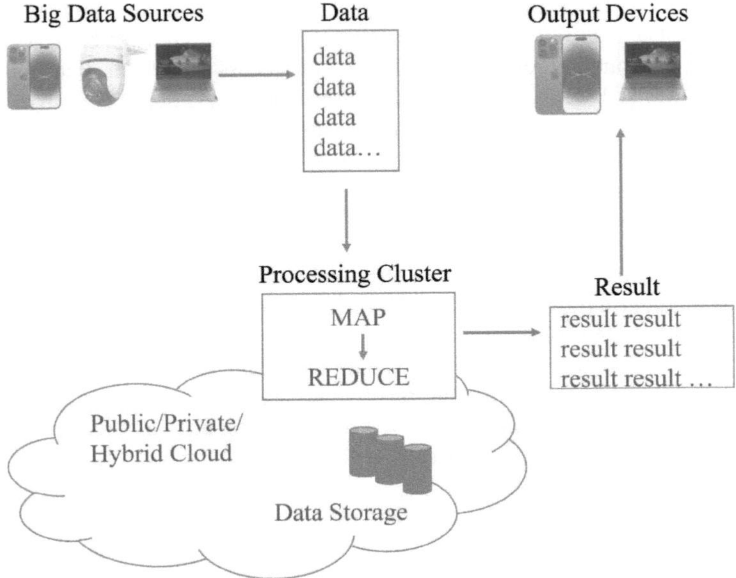

Figure 1 - Life cycle of big data

Security and privacy issues in the big data ecosystem:

- Insufficiently secured management interface: could allow an attacker to unauthorizedly exploit the administration interface (through cross-site scripting, cross-site query forgery and SQL injection, or other types of attacks) and gain unauthorized access to control the storage and processing device.
- Weak implementation of authentication/authorization mechanisms: could allow an attacker to exploit a bad password policy, crack weak passwords, and gain access to privileged modes.
- Using insecure or unnecessary network services: can lead to an attacker taking advantage of unnecessary or weak services running on the device, or using these services as a starting point to attack other devices on the network.
- Lack of transport encryption: allows an attacker to intercept data in transit between devices.
- Privacy concerns: arise because most devices collect users' personal data and do not adequately protect it.
- Insecure cloud interface: without proper controls, an attacker can use multiple attack vectors (authentication, lack of transport encryption, account enumeration) to access data or controls through a cloud resource.

- Insecure mobile interface: without proper controls, an attacker can use multiple attack vectors (authentication, lack of transport encryption, account enumeration) to access data or controls through the mobile interface using a variety of connection types.
- Insufficient granularity in security settings: due to missing or poor configuration mechanisms, an attacker can gain access to data or controls on the device.
- Insecure software/firmware: Attackers can take advantage of unencrypted and unauthenticated connections to intercept device updates and perform malicious updates that can compromise the device, the device network, and the data stored on it.
- Poor physical security: if an information processing device is physically accessible, an attacker could use USB ports, SD cards, or other storage to access the device's OS and possibly any data stored on the device.

As a result of the conducted work, the recommendations for the selection and application of methods were determined in relation to the banking sphere to minimize the risks and probability of occurrence of information security threats in the work with big data (Table 3):

Table 3- Recommendations for the selection and application of methods, as applied to the banking sector to minimize the risks and probability of information security threats in the work with big data.

Method	Method Description	Applicability in the banking process	Compliance	Way of realization	Type of protected information in banking activities	Recommendations
Risk management	Identify, assess and manage big data risks to ensure the security and continuit	Used for all processes related to data processing and big data analytics.	Complies with ISO 31000, ISO 27005 standards and requirements of the National Bank of the Republic of	1. risk identification: identify potential risks associated with the use of big data in banking	All types of data	Use risk management guidelines such as ISO 31000, ISO 27005. For initial

	y of business processes.		Kazakhstan (hereinafter - NBRK), ARRFR on risk management.	(data leaks, confidentiality breaches, unauthorized access, etc.). To implement this stage, it is necessary to conduct a preliminary inventory of data storage locations, make a list of types of processed data. 2. Risk analysis: analyze the probability and impact of each risk (use risk matrix methods). 3. Develop risk management strategies: select appropriate risk management techniques (avoid, mitigate, transfer, or accept		risk assessment cases, use simple qualitative or expert risk analysis methods; as the process matures, move to quantitative risk assessment. Use automation systems such as SAS Risk Management or IBM OpenPages. Conduct regular audits of the plan.

				risks).4. Documenting the risk management plan: create a plan with detailed risk management instructions.5. Implementing the risk management plan: assign responsibility for implementing the plan and communicating between participants.6. Monitoring and evaluating effectiveness: evaluate regularly and adjust the plan as needed.7. Ensure compliance: ensure that the plan complies with established internal and external		

				regulatory requirements, such as those of the NBK.		
Access control	Restrict access to data to authorized persons only to prevent unauthorized access.	Ensuring security of client data, restricting access to online banking systems and the bank's internal systems.	Complies with ISO/IEC 27001, ISO/IEC 27002, PCI DSS, NBRC, ARRF data security requirements, personal data protection legislation	1. Develop an access control policy: define user roles and rights, and describe the access control process (assigning, modifying, and removing access rights). 2. Adoption of multi-factor authentication (MFA): with numerous software vulnerabilities and improved attack methods against authentication and authorization	All types of data	Use identity and access management systems such as Okta or Microsoft Azure Active Directory. Conduct regular access control audits. Use the principles of "minimum sufficiency" and "just in time" when allocating access rights

				systems, the use of multi-factor authentication is the de facto required standard for all systems that handle sensitive data. 3. Identity and Access Management (IAM) systems: use enterprise user directories systems such as Okta or Microsoft Azure Active Directory to manage access rights, this reduces administrative errors by automating access management tasks. 4. Regular checks and audits: Control the list of accounts with		

				access and their authorization levels through periodic audits.		
Data encryption	Convert data into an encrypted format to ensure data confidentiality and integrity, using data hashing.	Protecting customer data in databases, securing online banking transactions, and controlling data integrity.	Complies with ISO/IEC 27002, NIST SP 800-53 and NBRC, ARRF data security and legal requirements for processing personal data.	1. define the data to be encrypted: define the data to be encrypted (e.g. sensitive personal data). 2. use strong encryption algorithms : e.g. AES-256 to ensure data security, consider legal restrictions on the choice of encryption algorithms and the import of cryptographic security features. 3. Implement encryption at different levels: use encryption at the	All types of data for which a breach of confidentiality poses unacceptable risks to the organization	Use strong encryption algorithms such as AES-256 and key management tools such as HashiCorp Vault. If you suspect that key information has been compromised, ensure that key information is changed in a timely manner, conduct routine key changes and re-encrypt data with new keys, encrypt data after the

				database, file, or network level. 4. Key Managem ent: Use key manageme nt tools such as HashiCorp Vault or HSM (Hardware Security Module) to manage encryption keys. 5. Ensure key security: update encryption keys regularly and store them securely.		terminati on of those who had access to it.
Data anony mizati on	Replacin g or deleting personal informati on from stored data to protect privacy.	Processi ng and analysis of clients' personal data, data related to various types of secrets (family, medical, tax, etc.). Ensuring confident iality of customer data during	Complies with the requirement s of the RK legislation on personal data protection and ISO/IEC 27018 standards for data protection in cloud services, IS requirement s of the NBRK and ARRFR.	1. Define the data to be anonymiz ed: Define the data to be anonymiz ed (e.g. personal data of customers). 2. Anonymiz ation methods: use anonymiz ation methods	Person al data, bankin g and other types of secrets protect ed by law	Conduct regular quality audits of anonymi zation and revise methods as needed. Use automati on tools to anonymi ze data.

		their analysis and processing		such as k-anonymity or l-diversity. 3. data anonymization tools: use programs such as K2VIEW, IBM InfoSphere Optim Data Privacy, Informatica Data Security Cloud, or Talend. 4. Check the quality of anonymization: test anonymization and security compliance regularly.			

Security monitoring	Monitor system events to detect and prevent security threats.	Monitoring of user and system activity. Information systems security control, detection and prevention of cyber threats.	Compliant with ISO/IEC 27001, ISO/IEC 27002 and complies with NBRK, ARRF data security requirements, PCI DSS.	1. Implement a security monitoring system: Use systems for collecting and correlating event logs (SIEM) to track user, administrator, and system activity. 2. Anomaly analysis and detection: Use programs to help identify anomalies, such as Splunk or Elastic SIEM. 3. Incident Response Plans: Develop plans in case security incidents are detected. 4. Regular monitoring and auditing: regularly check system activity and logs.	All types of data	Use security monitoring systems such as Splunk or Elastic SIEM. Conduct 24/7 monitoring and timely response to threats. Define a list of typical types of attacks on processed data and start monitoring with them; as other types of attacks are detected, add new monitoring rules to the list. Start monitoring with the most critical information systems of the company and gradually connect

				5. Timely response: Ensure prompt response to detected security threats.		other sources of event logs.
Data protection during transmission	Ensuring data security during transmission between systems and services.	Data protection during transfer between systems and services. Ensuring the security of customer data during its transfer between the bank's systems or during online transactions.	Compliant with ISO/IEC 27002, NIST SP 800-53 and complies with NBRC, ARRF data security, PCI DSS requirements.	1. use encryption protocols: use TLS/SSL to secure data transmission with key lengths appropriate to the current types of attacks on cryptographic algorithms, conduct annual checks of the cryptographic strength of the	All types of data	Use strong encryption protocols such as TLS/SSL to protect data in transit. Conduct penetration testing to identify vulnerabilities. Routinely change encryption keys for network communications.

				algorithms and encryption key lengths used. 2. Authentication: make sure that the data is authentic and the connection is secure. 3. penetration testing: conduct regular penetration testing to identify vulnerabilities. 4. Security Monitoring: Ensure that data transmission is monitored and audited to detect abnormal activity.		

Network segmentation	Split the network into subnets to improve security and isolate critical systems from attacks.	Network security and data protection.	Compliant with ISO/IEC 27002 standards and complies with NBRK, ARRF data security, PCI DSS requirements.	1. Identify network segments: Divide the network into segments based on data types, functions, and access rights. Separate test environments from production environments. Separate guest environments from internal environments. 2. Implement access control measures: Use firewalls, ACLs (access control lists), and other measures to restrict access between segments, such as 802.1X technology. 3. traffic monitoring: use systems to	All types of data	Use firewalls and ACLs to control access between network segments, apply network attack detection and prevention systems. Apply security measures for each segment.

				monitor and analyze traffic between network segments. 4. Segment security: Apply security measures for each network segment, such as encrypting data during transmission. 5. Provide isolation: isolate network segments from each other to prevent the spread of threats. 6. Use HoneyPot-type systems (traps) to detect unauthorized intrusion into isolated subnets.		

Incident Management	Plan and respond to security incidents to minimize damage and ensure business continuity.	Incident response and business continuity.	Compliant with ISO/IEC 27035, NIST SP 800-61 and complies with NBRC, ARRF Incident Management, and PCI DSS requirements.	1. Develop an incident management plan: create a plan with clear instructions on how to deal with certain types of incidents. 2. Assignment of Responsible Persons: Identify those responsible for responding to incidents. 3. Communicating the plan: make sure the plan is known to all staff and stakeholders. 4. staff training: provide training to incident responders. 5. Monitoring and evaluation	All types of data	Use ISO/IEC 27035 and NIST SP 800-61 to create an incident management plan. Conduct regular drills and exercises to practice the plan. Consider specific regulatory requirements for capturing information and notifying stakeholders, e.g., ARRF Board Resolution No. 90 of September 21, 2020. "On Approval of Requirements for Information Security Incident Response Services, Internal Investigations of

				: regularly review the effectiveness of the plan and revise it if necessary. 6. Regular drills and exercises: conduct practical drills to practice the plan.		Information Security Incidents"

Configuration management	Ensure system security and stability by managing settings and configurations.	Ensuring the stability and security of the system.	Compliant with ISO/IEC 27002 standards and complies with NBRK, ARRF configuration management, and PCI DSS requirements.	1. Identify key configuration elements: Identify critical system components such as servers, applications, and networks. 2. Define standards for secure configuration settings for different types of information assets (server, workstation, network equipment, etc.). 3. Implement automated configuration management systems, where applicable: use tools such as Ansible or Puppet for configuration management. 4. Regular checks and	All types of data	Use configuration management tools such as Ansible or Puppet. Conduct regular configuration checks and audits. Use vendor recommendations and international experts, such as the Center of Internet Security (CIS Benchmarks), when determining configuration standards

				audits: conduct regular checks and audits of the configuration to ensure compliance with standards. 5. Change Management: Use change management processes to control configuration changes. 6. Documentation: create and maintain system configuration documentation.		

Data Tokenization	Protect sensitive customer data such as card numbers and bank accounts by replacing them with tokens.	Protecting sensitive data such as customer financial information.	Compliant with NBRC requirements on personal data protection and PCI DSS standards.	1. Define the data to be tokenized: identify the sensitive data to be tokenized. 2. Implement tokenization: Use data tokenization systems such as Prime Factors EncryptRIGHT or CipherCloud. 3. token storage: ensure tokens are stored safely and in accordance with the original data. 4. Token access control: restrict access to tokens to authorized persons only. 5. Checking and testing: regularly check and test the	Financial information, personal data	Use data tokenization systems such as Prime Factors or CipherCloud. Conduct regular checks and testing of the tokenization system.

				tokenization system.		
Education and training	Provide knowledge and skills training to employees to raise awareness of data security practices.	Educate employees and raise their awareness of data security and new cyber defense techniques.	Compliant with NBRC, ARRF, PCI DSS training requirements and ISO/IEC 27001.	1. Develop a training program: Create a data security training program. 2. staff training: provide regular training to all staff, including training on how to prevent phishing and other threats. 3. Knowledge testing: test and validate employees' knowledg	All types of data	Establish a data security training program and provide regular training to all employees. Conduct knowledge checks and ensure the program is kept up-to-date.

				e of data security issues. 4. Keeping knowledge up-to-date: ensure that the training program is kept up-to-date in line with changes in legislation and threats.		
Security management	General organization of security measures and procedures for data protection.	Manage and ensure the security of all processes and data.	Compliant with ISO/IEC 27001, ISO/IEC 27002 and NBRK, ARRF, PCI DSS security management requirements.	1. Develop a security policy: create an information security policy in accordance with the requirements of the NBRC, ARRF and ISO/IEC 27001. 2. Organize security measures: Define security measures to protect data and processes. 3. Monitoring the implement	All types of data	Use ISO/IEC 27001 and ISO/IEC 27002 standards to organize security measures. Conduct regular reviews and audits. Establish a frequency and communicate to the organization's management the status and trends in

				ation of safety measures: designate those responsible for monitoring the implementation of safety measures. 4. Regular monitoring and auditing: conduct audits for compliance with the information security policy. 5. Business continuity: Create business continuity plans.		the maturity level of information security processes.

Protection against DDoS attacks	Preventing and mitigating distributed denial of service (DDoS) attacks.	Preventing denial of service attacks, protecting the bank's websites and online services.	Meets NIST SP 800-63-3 standards, NBRC requirements, ARRFR, and ENISA recommendations.	1. Implement DDoS protection solutions: Use specialized software or hardware DDoS protection tools such as Cloudflare, Akamai, Radware. Alternatively, purchase network traffic scrubbing services from network service providers. Adjust network equipment and web server configurations to reduce the likelihood of successful attacks on network-accessible Internet resources by setting limits on the number of network connections and	All types of data	Use DdoS protection solutions such as Cloudflare, Akamai, Radware, F5. Conduct traffic monitoring and analysis to detect DdoS attacks.

				requests per unit of time. 2. Monitor and analyze traffic: Monitor and analyze traffic to detect DdoS attacks. 3. DdoS attack response plans: Develop DdoS attack response plans. 4. Ensure redundancy: Ensure systems are redundant to mitigate the effects of attacks. 5. Ensure communication: inform clients about possible problems during DdoS attacks.		

Ensuring confidentiality	Protecting the confidentiality of personal data of clients and employees.	Processing and storage of personal data of customers and employees.	Complies with the requirements of the RK legislation on personal data protection and GDPR standard.	1. Identify the data to be protected: Identify the personal data of customers and employees to be protected. 2. Develop a privacy policy: create a privacy policy in accordance with the requirements of the RK legislation and GDPR standard. 3 Ensure customer consent: ensure that customers have consented to the processing of their personal data for the required list of processing purposes. 4. Data minimization: limit the	Personal data, employee data	Create a privacy policy in accordance with the requirements of the RK legislation and GDPR standard. Ensure minimization of stored and processed data and transparency of data processing.

				collection and storage of data to the extent necessary only for the fulfillment of the processing purposes set out in the consents of personal data subjects. 5. Data protection: Use encryption, tokenization and other measures to protect data. 6. Ensure transparency: provide customers with information on how their data is processed.		

Chang e control	Manage changes to systems and processes to ensure data security and integrity.	Ensure data security and integrity as systems and processe s change.	Complies with ISO/IEC 27002 and NBRK, ARRFR change managemen t requirement s.	1 Define a change manageme nt process: Establish a change manageme nt process for systems and processes. Consider the risks inherent in the change, and for changes with high informatio n security risks, provide detailed plans for undoing the change. 2. Implement change manageme nt tools: Use tools such as Jira or ServiceNo w to track changes. 3. Change testing: analyze and test changes before implement ation. 4. Document ing	All types of data	Use change managem ent tools such as Jira or ServiceN ow. Conduct regular change checks and process audits.

				changes: Document all changes for tracking purposes. 5. Regular audits: conduct regular audits of the change management process.		
Data masking	Replacing real data with pseudonyms or altered data to protect privacy.	Processing and analyzing customers' personal data.	Compliant with ISO/IEC 27018 and complies with NBRC, ARRF data protection requirements.	1. define the data to be masked: define the data to be masked (e.g. personal data of customers). 2. Masking techniques: Use masking techniques such as character substitution or data ranges. 3. data masking tools: use programs such as	Personal data	Use data masking programs such as Informatica or Delphix. Perform regular checks and tests of the quality of masking.

				Informatica or Delphix to automate data masking. 4. Inspection and testing: regularly check the quality of the masking and its compliance with safety requirements.		
Creation of policies and internal documents	Develop policies and procedures to ensure security and compliance.	Creating documents to manage data security.	Compliant with ISO/IEC 27001, ISO/IEC 27002 and complies with NBRK, ARRF, PCI DSS requirements.	1. Development of security policies: create information security policy and downstream regulations and instructions in accordance with the requirements of the RK regulatory acts and ISO/IEC 27001, PCI DSS standards .2 Create internal documents : prepare	All types of data	Create security policy and internal documents in accordance with the requirements of RoK legislation and international standards. Conduct regular audits and update documents.

				documents such as user manuals, safety standards and procedures. 3. Communication of policies and documents: make sure that policies and documents are known to all employees. 4. enforce policies: conduct regular audits to ensure compliance with established security requirements. 5. Update and review: regularly review and update policies and documents.		

5 TESTING AND SECURITY ASSESSMENT OF BIG DATA PROCESSING AND STORAGE SYSTEMS

5.1 Preparing test scenarios to evaluate the security of big data processing and storage systems

Testing and evaluating the effectiveness of security techniques in big data are important steps in the design and application of big data processing and storage systems. In this section, we review the main aspects of preparing test scenarios to evaluate the security of such systems.

The first step in preparing test scenarios is to define the goals and security requirements of the big data processing and storage system. This may include requirements for data confidentiality, data integrity, data availability, user authentication and authorization, and protection against external attacks.

Next, a system vulnerability analysis should be performed and potential vulnerabilities that could be exploited by attackers to breach data security should be identified. This may include analyzing vulnerabilities in the operating system, databases, network protocols, and big data processing and storage system software.

Based on vulnerability analysis, test scenarios should be developed to evaluate the effectiveness of big data security practices. Test scenarios may include simulating attacks, verifying the presence and correct implementation of authentication and authorization mechanisms, as well as verifying the presence and correct implementation of encryption and data access control mechanisms.

One important aspect of preparing test scenarios is selecting the right data sets for testing. The data should be representative of the real-world use cases of the big data system and security tools. This can include data of different types such as text, numeric, audio, and video data, as well as data of different formats such as tables, documents, images, and video files. For example, for testing anti-virus products, test suites of test programs that are recognized by anti-viruses as a virus are used. When testing network filtering tools, a set of protocols and programs that provide a variety of methods of obfuscation (hiding) of data is prepared. When testing systems to combat information leakage, sets of files or keywords are prepared, which are used to test the level of effectiveness of detection of attempts to steal data.

In general, various aspects of data security should be considered when developing test scenarios. For example, you can check how the system processes and stores data in encrypted form and what data access control mechanisms are implemented. You can also test how the system responds to unauthorized data access attempts or denial of service attacks.

Various tools and technologies can be used to conduct test scenarios. For example, specialized tools can be used to scan for system vulnerabilities, as well as tools to simulate attacks. You can also use tools to monitor and analyze network traffic to identify unauthorized attempts to access data.

After running the test scenarios, it is necessary to analyze the results obtained and evaluate the effectiveness of security practices in big data. It is important to take into account that system security testing is an ongoing process, and test results may change over time. Therefore, it is recommended to regularly test and evaluate the security of the big data processing and storage system.

The first step in testing is to prepare the test environment. For this purpose, it is necessary to select a set of real data that will be used in the testing process. In the banking industry, this could be data on customers, transactions, accounts and other financial operations. It is important to make sure that the selected data corresponds to real-life usage scenarios and allows to evaluate the effectiveness of security methods in real-life conditions.

Next, it is necessary to define criteria for evaluating the effectiveness of security methods. The criteria may include such parameters as speed of data processing, reliability of protection against unauthorized access, resistance to attacks, ease of use, etc.

After preparing the test environment and defining the evaluation criteria, you can begin testing the security methods. During the testing process, different data usage scenarios should be used to evaluate the effectiveness of the techniques in different situations. For example, you can test how a security method handles the processing of large amounts of data or real-time protection against attacks.

Once the testing is complete, it is necessary to analyze the results obtained and draw conclusions about the effectiveness and reliability of the applied security methods in big data. It is important to take into account all identified problems and vulnerabilities in order to develop recommendations for their elimination and improvement. It is also possible to compare the test results with the security requirements in the banking industry and determine whether the security methods meet these requirements.

Thus, testing of security methods on real data in the banking industry allows to assess the effectiveness and reliability of methods in real conditions, to identify potential vulnerabilities and problems, as well as to develop recommendations for their elimination and improvement. Testing on real data in the banking sector allows to evaluate more accurately the effectiveness of security methods and apply them in practice.

5.2 Testing approaches for assessing the security of big data processing and storage systems

The following approaches can be used to test security techniques in big data:

1- Threat Model Testing. In this case, potential threats to data security are identified and modeled to assess the effectiveness of security practices in preventing or minimizing the impact of these threats.

2- Scenario-based testing. In this case, attack scenarios that could be used to gain unauthorized access to data are developed. Security techniques are then tested for their effectiveness in preventing or detecting such attacks. The MITRE ATT&CK methodology [39] is widely used to catalog different types of attacks into components and improve the effectiveness of measures aimed at preventing the implementation of a particular type of attack.

3. load-based testing. In this case, security methods are tested for their effectiveness in dealing with large amounts of data and high processing speeds. In this case, load tests are created that simulate real data handling conditions.

4. vulnerability-based testing. This involves analyzing the vulnerabilities of security practices and exploiting them to assess their effectiveness in preventing or detecting such vulnerabilities.

After testing, it is necessary to analyze the results obtained and evaluate the effectiveness of security techniques in big data. For this purpose, the following aspects should be taken into account:

1. Compliance with security requirements. The assessment of the effectiveness of security methods should be based on their compliance with the security requirements established in the banking sector of the Republic of Kazakhstan. It is important to make sure that security methods provide the necessary level of data protection and comply with the legislation.

2. Reliability and stability of operation. An evaluation of the effectiveness of security practices should include an analysis of their reliability and stability. It is important to ensure that the security practices operate without disruption and that the level of adverse impact on the performance of the data processing system is acceptable.

3. Protection against threats. Evaluating the effectiveness of security practices should include an analysis of their protection against various data security threats. It is important to ensure that security practices effectively prevent unauthorized access to data and ensure its confidentiality and integrity.

4. Performance and scalability. Evaluating the effectiveness of security practices should include an analysis of their performance and scalability. It is important to ensure that the security practices do not significantly degrade the performance of the data processing system and can scale with increasing data volumes.

CONCLUSION

In this paper the issues related to the security of Big Data processing (Big Data) in the banking sector of the Republic of Kazakhstan were considered. Introduction to the problematics of security in Big Data allowed to familiarize with the main aspects of this problem, as well as with the relevance and significance of this topic.

Within the framework of the research various methods of big data security were considered. The main approaches to data encryption, user authentication and authorization, data access control, as well as methods of detecting and preventing attacks on big data systems were studied, and organizational measures aimed at reducing information security risks when working with big data were given.

For a more complete understanding of the situation in the banking sector of the Republic of Kazakhstan, a review of existing regulatory acts and international standards of information security was conducted. National and international standards that regulate security issues in the banking sector were considered. Problems related to the application of regulatory acts and standards in the context of big data were also noted.

One of the main results of the work is the development of recommendations to ensure security in big data for the banking sector of the Republic of Kazakhstan. The main requirements to data security were defined, and methods and measures to ensure them were proposed. The developed recommendations can be used by the banks of the Republic of Kazakhstan to improve the level of security of their systems of processing and storage of big data.

In order to verify the effectiveness of the developed security methods, testing and evaluation methods for the effectiveness of the security measures were analyzed. Appropriate evaluation criteria were selected and guidance was provided for determining test methods.

Implementation of the developed recommendations in the banking sector of the Republic of Kazakhstan is beyond the scope of this paper. For successful implementation it is necessary to conduct personnel training, as well as to adapt the developed recommendations to the specific conditions and requirements of the banking sector. Implementation of the developed standards will allow the banks of the Republic of Kazakhstan to increase the level of security of their systems of processing and storage of big data, as well as to provide more effective protection of confidentiality and integrity of data.

In conclusion, it can be noted that ensuring security in the field of big data is an urgent and complex problem that requires constant attention and development. Development of standards and recommendations for ensuring security in big data for the banking sector of the Republic of

Kazakhstan is an important step in solving this problem. However, it should be taken into account that security in the field of big data is a dynamic area, and therefore the developed standards and recommendations should be constantly updated and adapted to changing conditions and threats.

REFERENCE LIST

1. Kozlova N. P. Use of Big Data Technologies in the Financial Industry // Economic Systems. 2020. №4. URL: [https://cyberleninka.ru/article/n/ispolzovanie-tehnologiy-big-data-v-finansovoy-otrasli] (date of reference: 18.03.2024).
2. Nurgaliev R. A. Impact of digital corruption on the global community: problems and methods of struggle. - 2022. URL: https://repository.apa.kz/bitstream/handle/123456789/939/6 Nurgaliev Rakhat.pdf?sequence=1&isAllowed=y (date of reference: 14.01.2024).
3. "Assessment of cyber risks in banks in Kazakhstan", June 2021, Deloitte e with the support of the Agency of the Republic of Kazakhstan on Regulation and Development of Financial Market URL: https://www2.deloitte.com/content/dam/Deloitte/kz/Documents/risk/2021/%D0%9E%D1%86%D0%B5%D0%BD%D0%BA%D0%B0%20%D0%BA%D0%B8%D0%B1%D0%B5%D1%80%D1%80%D0%B8%D1%81%D0%BA%D0%BE%D0%B2%20%D0%91%D0%B0%D0%BD%D0%BA%D0%BE%D0%B2%20%D0%9A%D0%B0%D0%B7%D0%B0%D1%85%D1%81%D1%82%D0%B0%D0%BD%D0%B0-%D0%9E%D1%82%D1%87%D0%B5%D1%82%20%D0%94%D0%B5%D0%BB%D0%BE%D0%B9%D1%82%D0%B0.pdf (accessed 15.04.2024);
4. On Approval of the Data Management Requirements. URL: https://adilet.zan.kz/rus/docs/V2200030186 (date of circulation 01.02.2024)
5. Ermolaev K. N., Musabekov O. U. BBC U01, U05, A3, CH4, A9 TS75. - 2020.URL: https://naucorp.ru/upload/iblock/095/ft98w90d0tecghxe2g5rxqv0gj6umr28/MONOGRAFIYA-KM_12_20-_set_.pdf (date of reference: 17.01.2024).
6. Talapina E. V. Protection of personal data in the digital era: Russian law in the European context // Proceedings of the Institute of State and Law of the Russian Academy of Sciences. - 2018. - T. 13. - №. 5. - C. 117-150. URL: https://cyberleninka.ru/article/n/zaschita-personalnyh-dannyh-v-tsifrovuyu-epohu-rossiyskoe-pravo-v-evropeyskom-kontekste (date of access: 08.02.2024).
7. Koval K. V. Problems of bank financing of innovations // Vestnik of Modern Research. - 2018. - №. 7.2. - C. 103-106. URL: http://portfolio.vvsu.ru/files/013B6DF7-E4F6-49EF-8FD7-B39A0E81FC24.pdf#page=103 (date of reference: 03.02.2024).
8. Pasinitskaya A. D. Digitalization in international retail banking business: state and prospects of development: thesis. - 2022.

URL: https://elib.bsu.by/handle/123456789/282993 (date of reference: 17.02.2024).

9. Global Cyber Security Index URL: https://composite-indicators.jrc.ec.europa.eu/explorer/explorer/indices/GCI/global-cyber-security-index (accessed 17.02.2024).

10. Report on activity of the Agency of RK on regulation and development of the financial market for 2022 URL: https://www.gov.kz/memleket/entities/ardfm/documents/details/501699?lang=ru (date of address 01.05.2024).

11. Martynenko N. N., Kotova E. O. Analytics and forecasts of the introduction of cloud technologies and big data in the activities of banks in an unstable economy // Financial Markets and Banks. 2022. №5. URL: https://cyberleninka.ru/article/n/analitika-i-prognozy-vnedreniya-oblachnyh-tehnologiy-i-big-data-v-deyatelnosti-bankov-v-usloviyah-nestabilnoy-ekonomiki (date of access: 14.01.2024).

12. Shaidullina V. K. Big data and personal data protection: the main problems of theory and practice of legal regulation // Society: politics, economics, law. 2019. №1 (66). URL: https://cyberleninka.ru/article/n/bolshie-dannye-i-zaschita-personalnyh-dannyh-osnovnye-problemy-teorii-i-praktiki-pravovogo-regulirovaniya (date of reference: 11.03.2024).

13. Kirin D. A. A., Saakov V. V., Aghajanyan E. Yu. Big data processing systems for human labor reduction // Student Scientific Research: Collection of Articles X. - 2022. - C. 59. URL: https://naukaip.ru/wp-content/uploads/2022/02/MK-1312.pdf#page=59 (date of reference: 18.03.2024).

14. Denisova O. Yu. Yu., Mukhutdinov E.A. Big data is not only the size of data // Bulletin of Kazan Technological University. 2015. №4. URL: https://cyberleninka.ru/article/n/bolshie-dannye-eto-ne-tolko-razmer-dannyh (date of reference: 02.04.2024).

15. Introduction to Transparent Data Encryption URL: https://docs.oracle.com/en/database/oracle/oracle-database/12.2/asoag/introduction-to-transparent-data-encryption.html (accessed 02.04.2024).

16. Astapenko T. S., Sokolin D. D. Security problems of the Hadoop big data processing system // Reshetnev Readings. 2018. №. URL: https://cyberleninka.ru/article/n/problemy-bezopasnosti-sistemy-obrabotki-bolshih-dannyh-hadoop (date of reference: 09.02.2024).

17. Polyanin A.V., Dolgova S.A. Modern trends of e-business in the banking sector // EGI. 2018. №3 (21). URL: https://cyberleninka.ru/article/n/sovremennye-tendentsii-elektronnogo-biznesa-v-bankovskom-sektore (date of access: 10.03.2024).

18. Kulikova O. M. M., Tropynina N. E. Problems of using big data technology in modern market conditions // Innovative economy:

prospects of development and improvement. 2022. №7 (65). URL: https://cyberleninka.ru/article/n/problemy-ispolzovaniya-tehnologii-big-data-v-sovremennyh-rynochnyh-usloviyah (date of reference: 18.03.2024).

19. On Approval of the Requirements for ensuring information security of banks, branches of non-resident banks of the Republic of Kazakhstan and organizations engaged in certain types of banking operations, Rules and terms of providing information on information security incidents, including information on violations, failures in information systems. URL: https://adilet.zan.kz/rus/docs/V1800016772 (circulation date: 18.03.2024).

20. Ivanov K. V., Balyakin A. A., Malyshev A. S. Big data technologies as a tool to ensure national security // π-Economy. 2020. №1. URL: https://cyberleninka.ru/article/n/tehnologii-bolshih-dannyh-kak-instrument-obespecheniya-natsionalnoy-bezopasnosti (date of address: 18.03.2024).

21. ST RK ISO/IEC 27001-2015 "Information technology. Methods and means of ensuring security. Information security management systems. Requirements" URL: https://online.zakon.kz/Document/?doc_id=36588184 (date of circulation: 01.05.2024)

22. NIST SP 800-53 Rev. 5 "Security and Privacy Controls for Information Systems and Organizations" URL: https://csrc.nist.gov/pubs/sp/800/53/r5/upd1/final (accessed 01.05.2024)

23. Swift Customer Security Controls Framework URL: https://www.swift.com/ru/node/300801(accessed 08.04.2024)

24. Dolzhikova A. E., Sembekova B. R., Yasin M. Regulation of big data application in the Republic of Korea and Russia // Vestnik of SPbSU. Series 14. Law. 2022. №1. URL: https://cyberleninka.ru/article/n/regulirovanie-primeneniya-bolshihdannyh-v-respublike-koreya-i-rossii (date of address: 18.03.2024).

25. Requirements for ensuring information security of banks, branches of non-resident banks of the Republic of Kazakhstan and organizations engaged in certain types of banking operations, approved by Resolution of the Board of the ARRFR No. 48 dated 27.03.2018.

26. CIS Critical Security Controls. URL: https://www.cisecurity.org/controls/v8_pre (accessed 19.03.2024).

27. Kazpost database with customer data offered for sale on hacker site URL: https://kaztag.kz/en/news/kazpost-database-with-customer-data-offered-for-sale-on-hacker-site- (date of address: 18.03.2024).

28. Information portal polisia.kz URL: https://polisia.kz/ru/v-almaty-proshla-spetsoperatsiya-po-zaderzhaniyu-krupnogo-hakera/ (date of reference: 18.03.2024).

29. Analysis of Spear Phishing threat to RK banking segment URL: https://tntsecure.kz/en/lokibot.html (date of access: 18.03.2024).

30. Almaty City Prosecutor's Office URL: https://www.gov.kz/memleket/entities/prokuratura-almaty/press/news/details/210761?lang=ru (date of reference: 18.03.2024).

31. On realization of operational risk in the Bank URL: https://t.me/risktakerskz/1430 (access date: 18.03.2024).

32. Computer Incident Response Service Statistics. URL: https://lsm.kz/hakery-chashe-vsego-atakuyut-finsektor-i-gosorgany-kazahstana (date of access: 18.03.2024).

33. Information security in the financial market. URL: https://bizmedia.kz/2023-12-25-informaczionnaya-bezopasnost-na-finansovom-rynke-chto-nuzhno-znat-kazahstanczam/ (date of reference: 18.03.2024).

34. Resolution of the ARFMR Board No. 89 dated September 21, 2020. "On Approval of Requirements for Competencies of Heads and Employees of Information Security Units, Including Requirements for Professional Development of Persons Responsible for Information Security".

35. Concerning the Approval of Requirements for the Competencies of Heads and Employees of Information Security Units, Including Requirements for the Professional Development of Persons Responsible for Information Security. URL: https://adilet.zan.kz/rus/docs/V2000021251 (access date: 18.03.2024).

36. Orlov G. A., Krasov A. A. V., Gelfand A. M. Application of big data in analyzing big data in computer networks // Science-intensive technologies in space research of the Earth. 2020. №4. URL: https://cyberleninka.ru/article/n/primenenie-big-data-pri-analize-bolshih-dannyh-v-kompyuternyh-setyah (date of address: 19.03.2024).

37. Martynenko N. N., Kotova E. O. Analytics and forecasts of the introduction of cloud technologies and big data in the activities of banks in an unstable economy // Financial Markets and Banks. 2022. №5. URL: https://cyberleninka.ru/article/n/analitika-i-prognozy-vnedreniya-oblachnyh-tehnologiy-i-big-data-v-deyatelnosti-bankov-v-usloviyah-nestabilnoy-ekonomiki (date of access: 19.03.2024).

38. OWASP Data Security Top 10. URL: https://owasp.org/www-project-data-security-top-10/ (accessed 19.03.2024).

39. ATT&CK Matrix for Enterprise. URL: https://attack.mitre.org/(date of access: 27.03.2024).

Appendix A - List of regulatory legal acts and laws of the Republic of Kazakhstan in the sphere of information security of the financial market.

Insurance organizations
Decision of the Board of Directors (hereinafter - the BoD) of the NBRK No. 14 dated January 28, 2016. "On Approval of the Rules for Determining the Amount of Damage Caused to a Vehicle"
PP ARRFR No. 67 dated September 12, 2022 "On Approval of the Rules for Connection and Use by Financial Institutions of the Informatization Object for Collection, Processing and Exchange of Information on Information Security Events and Incidents Used by the Sectoral Information Security Center of the Financial Market and Financial Institutions"
PP ARRFR No. 110 dated November 23, 2020. "On Approval of the Rules for Assessing the Level of Protection against Information Security Threats"
PP ARRFR No. 111 dated November 23, 2020. "On Approval of the Information Security Risk Assessment Methodology, Including the Procedure for Ranking Financial Organizations by the Degree of Exposure to Information Security Risks"
PP NBRK No. 164 of 10.07.2018. "On Approval of the Requirements for the organization of secure work ensuring safety and protection of information from unauthorized access to data stored in the insurance (reinsurance) organization, as well as cybersecurity of the insurance (reinsurance) organization"
PP AFN No. 177 of 25.06.2007. "On Approval of the Requirements for the Organization's Activities on Formation and Maintenance of the Database"
PP NBRK No. 259 dated October 29, 2018. "On Approval of the Rules of placing information on the Internet resource of an insurance organization, insurance broker, branch of an insurance (reinsurance) organization - non-resident of the Republic of Kazakhstan, branch of an insurance broker - non-resident of the Republic of Kazakhstan, organization guaranteeing insurance payments to insureds (insured, beneficiaries) in case of forced liquidation of insurance organizations, branches of insurance (reinsurance) organizations - non-residents of the Republic of Kazakhstan, insurance ombudsman, organization for insurance and reinsurance organizations - non-residents of the Republic of Kazakhstan".
Microfinance organizations
PP ARRFR No. 67 dated September 12, 2022 "On Approval of the Rules for Connection and Use by Financial Institutions of the Informatization Object for Collection, Processing and Exchange of Information on Information Security Events and Incidents Used by the Sectoral Information Security Center of the Financial Market and Financial Institutions"
PP ARRFR No. 110 dated November 23, 2020. "On Approval of the Rules for Assessing the Level of Protection against Information Security Threats"

PP ARRFR No. 111 dated November 23, 2020. "On Approval of the Information Security Risk Assessment Methodology, Including the Procedure for Ranking Financial Organizations by the Degree of Exposure to Information Security Risks"
PP NBK No. 217 of 28.11.2019. "On Approval of the Rules for granting microcredits electronically"
PP NBRK No. 228 dated 27.09.2018. "On Approval of the Requirements for the Use of Information and Communication Technologies and Information Security in Organizing the Activities of Credit Bureaus, Information Providers and Recipients of Credit Reports Being Banks, Organizations Engaged in Certain Types of Banking Operations, Microfinance Organizations and Collection Agencies, as well as Requirements to be Demanded by Credit Bureaus to Information Providers and Recipients of Credit Reports Pursuant to Subparagraph 11) of Paragraph 2 and Subparagraph 9) of Paragraph 3 of c
Organizations performing cash currency exchange activities
PP NBRK № 20 of February 28, 2022 "On Approval of Requirements for Internal Control Rules to Combat Money Laundering and Terrorist Financing for legal entities operating exclusively through exchange bureaus on the basis of the license of the National Bank of the Republic of Kazakhstan for exchange operations with cash foreign currency, and legal entities whose exclusive activity is the collection of banknotes, coins and valuables".
PP NBRK №49 of April 4, 2019. "On Approval of the Rules for Execution of Exchange Operations with Foreign Currency in Cash in the Republic of Kazakhstan"
PP NBK #91 of July 20, 2020. "On approval of the list, forms and terms of reporting on compliance with the requirements of the legislation of the Republic of Kazakhstan on combating legalization (laundering) of proceeds of crime and financing of terrorism by a legal entity operating exclusively through an exchange office under the license of the National Bank of the Republic of Kazakhstan for exchange operations with foreign currency in cash, and the Rules of its submission".
Payment organizations
PP NBK No. 200 dated August 31, 2016. "On Approval of the Requirements to Organizational Measures and Software and Hardware Means Ensuring Access to Payment Systems".
PP NBRK No. 202 dated August 31, 2016. "On Approval of the Rules for the Issue, Use and Redemption of Electronic Money, as well as Requirements to the Issuers of Electronic Money and Electronic Money Systems in the Territory of the Republic of Kazakhstan".
PP NBK No. 215 of August 31, 2016 "On Approval of the Rules for Organization of Payment Institutions' Activities"
Laws

Law "On State Regulation, Control and Supervision of the Financial Market and Financial Organizations"
Law "On currency regulation and currency control"
Law "On Banks and Banking Activity in the Republic of Kazakhstan"
Law "On Credit Bureaus and Formation of Credit Histories in the Republic of Kazakhstan"
Law "On the National Bank of the Republic of Kazakhstan"
Law "On Collection Activity"
Law "On the Securities Market"
Law "On Microfinance Activity"
Law "On Insurance Activities"
Law "On Payments and Payment Systems"
Banks
PP NBRK No. 11 dated February 28, 2022 "On Approval of the Requirements to the Internal Control Rules for Combating Money Laundering, Financing of Terrorism and Financing Weapons of Mass Destruction Proliferation for Payment Institutions".
PP NBRK № 14 of February 24, 2020. "On approval of the Rules of organization of security and device of premises of second-tier banks, branches of non-resident banks of the Republic of Kazakhstan, the National Postal Operator, legal entities whose exclusive activity is the collection of banknotes, coins and valuables, and legal entities operating exclusively through exchange offices on the basis of the license of the National Bank of the Republic of Kazakhstan for exchange operations with cash foreign currency"
PP NBRK No. 34 dd. 28.01.2016. "On Approval of Requirements for Security and Continuity of Operation of Information Systems of Banks and Organizations Engaged in Certain Types of Banking Operations".
PP ARRFR No. 36 dated March 30, 2020. "On approval of the Rules for issuance of permission to open a bank, branch of a non-resident bank of the Republic of Kazakhstan and grounds for refusal to issue permission to open a bank, Rules for licensing of banks, branches of non-resident banks of the Republic of Kazakhstan to conduct banking and other operations stipulated by the banking legislation of the Republic of Kazakhstan, licensing for banking and other operations carried out by Islamic banks, branches of non-resident Islamic banks of the Republic of Kazakhstan".
PP NBRK No. 47 dd. 27.03.2018. "On Approval of the Rules and Terms of Submission by Banks of Information Security Management Systems Availability and Compliance with Information Security Requirements to the National Information Security Coordination Center".

PP NBRK No. 48 dd. 27.03.2018. "On Approval of the Requirements for Ensuring Information Security of Banks and Organizations Engaged in Certain Types of Banking Operations, Rules and Terms of Providing Information on Information Security Incidents, Including Information on Violations, Failures in Information Systems"
PP NBRK №49 of April 4, 2019. "On Approval of the Rules for Execution of Exchange Operations with Foreign Currency in Cash in the Republic of Kazakhstan"
PP NBRK No. 64 dated April 10, 2019. "On Approval of the Rules for Monitoring Currency Transactions in the Republic of Kazakhstan"
PP ARRFR No. 67 dated September 12, 2022 "On Approval of the Rules for Connection and Use by Financial Institutions of the Informatization Object for Collection, Processing and Exchange of Information on Information Security Events and Incidents Used by the Sectoral Information Security Center of the Financial Market and Financial Institutions"
PP ARRFR No. 89 dated September 21, 2020. "On Approval of Requirements for the Competencies of Heads and Employees of Information Security Units, Including Requirements for Professional Development of Persons Responsible for Information Security".
PP ARRFR No. 90 dated September 21, 2020. "On Approval of Requirements for Information Security Incident Response Services, Internal Investigations of Information Security Incidents".
PP ARRFR No. 110 dated November 23, 2020. "On Approval of the Rules for Assessing the Level of Protection against Information Security Threats"
PP ARRFR No. 111 dated November 23, 2020. "On Approval of the Information Security Risk Assessment Methodology, Including the Procedure for Ranking Financial Organizations by the Degree of Exposure to Information Security Risks"
PP NBRK №120 dated September 28, 2020. "On Approval of the Rules for Cash Operations with Individuals and Legal Entities in the National Bank of the Republic of Kazakhstan".
PP NBRK No. 188 of 12.11.2019. "On Approval of the Rules for Formation of Risk Management and Internal Control System for Second-tier Banks"
PP NBK No. 200 dated August 31, 2016. "On Approval of the Requirements to Organizational Measures and Software and Hardware Means Ensuring Access to Payment Systems".
PP NBRK No. 201 dated August 31, 2016. "On Approval of the Rules of Operation of the Interbank Money Transfer System"
PP NBRK No. 202 dated August 31, 2016. "On Approval of the Rules of issue, use and redemption of e-money, as well as requirements to e-money issuers and e-money systems in the territory of the Republic of Kazakhstan".
PP NBRK No. 205 dated August 31, 2016. "On Approval of the Rules for issuance of payment cards, as well as requirements to the activity on servicing transactions with their use in the territory of the Republic of Kazakhstan".

PP NBRK No. 207 dated August 31, 2016. "On Approval of the Rules for Opening, Maintaining and Closing Bank Accounts of Customers"
PP NBRK #208 dated August 31, 2016 "On Approval of the Rules for Non-cash Payments and (or) Money Transfers on the Territory of the Republic of Kazakhstan"
PP NBRK No. 211 dated August 31, 2016. "On Approval of the Rules of Operation of the Interbank Clearing System"
PP NBRK No. 212 dated August 31, 2016. "On Approval of the Rules for Provision of Electronic Banking Services by Banks and Organizations Engaged in Certain Types of Banking Operations".
PP NBRK No. 216 dated August 31, 2016. "On Approval of the Rules for Interbank Payments and (or) Money Transfers on Transactions with Payment Cards in the Republic of Kazakhstan".
PP NBK No. 217 of August 31, 2016. "On Approval of the Rules of Functioning of the Interbank Payment Card System".
PP NBRK No. 228 dated 27.09.2018. "On Approval of the Requirements for the Use of Information and Communication Technologies and Ensuring Information Security in Organizing the Activities of Credit Bureaus, Information Providers and Recipients of Credit Reports Being Banks, Organizations Performing Certain Types of Banking Operations, Microfinance Organizations and Collection Agencies, as well as Requirements to be Demanded by Credit Bureaus to Information Providers and Recipients of Credit Reports Pursuant to Subparagraph 11) of Paragraph 2 and Subparagraph 9) of Paragraph 3 of c
Securities market
PP ARRFR No. 67 dated September 12, 2022 "On Approval of the Rules for Connection and Use by Financial Institutions of the Informatization Object for Collection, Processing and Exchange of Information on Information Security Events and Incidents Used by the Sectoral Information Security Center of the Financial Market and Financial Institutions"
PP ARRFR No. 90 dated September 21, 2020. "On Approval of Requirements for Information Security Incident Response Services, Internal Investigations of Information Security Incidents".
PP ARRFR No. 110 dated November 23, 2020. "On Approval of the Rules for Assessing the Level of Protection against Information Security Threats"
PP ARRFR No. 111 dated November 23, 2020. "On Approval of the Information Security Risk Assessment Methodology, Including the Procedure for Ranking Financial Organizations by the Degree of Exposure to Information Security Risks"
PP NBRK No. 165 of 28.04.2012. "On Approval of Requirements for Software and Hardware and Other Equipment Necessary for Activities on the Securities Market".
PP NBRK No. 318 of December 28, 2018. "On Approval of the Rules for Formation of Risk Management and Internal Control System for the Central Securities Depository"

Collection organizations
PP ARRFR No. 61 dated September 12, 2022 "On Approval of Requirements for Bank Subsidiaries Acquiring Doubtful and Uncollectible Assets of the Parent Bank and Collection Agencies Acting as Service Companies to Which the Rights (Claims) under Bank Loan Agreements and (or) Microcredit Agreements May Be Transferred to Trust Management".
Credit bureaus
PP NBRK No. 228 dated 27.09.2018. "On Approval of the Requirements for the Use of Information and Communication Technologies and Ensuring Information Security in Organizing the Activities of Credit Bureaus, Information Providers and Recipients of Credit Reports Being Banks, Organizations Performing Certain Types of Banking Operations, Microfinance Organizations and Collection Agencies, as well as Requirements to be Demanded by Credit Bureaus to Information Providers and Recipients of Credit Reports Pursuant to Subparagraph 11) of Paragraph 2 and Subparagraph 9) of Paragraph 3 of c
Organizations performing certain types of banking operations
PP NBRK No. 34 dd. 28.01.2016. "On Approval of Requirements for Security and Continuity of Operation of Information Systems of Banks and Organizations Engaged in Certain Types of Banking Operations".
PP NBRK No. 48 dd. 27.03.2018. "On Approval of the Requirements for Ensuring Information Security of Banks and Organizations Engaged in Certain Types of Banking Operations, Rules and Terms of Providing Information on Information Security Incidents, Including Information on Violations, Failures in Information Systems"
PP ARRFR No. 67 dated September 12, 2022 "On Approval of the Rules for Connection and Use by Financial Institutions of the Informatization Object for Collection, Processing and Exchange of Information on Information Security Events and Incidents Used by the Sectoral Information Security Center of the Financial Market and Financial Institutions"
PP ARRFR No. 90 dated September 21, 2020. "On Approval of Requirements for Information Security Incident Response Services, Internal Investigations of Information Security Incidents".
PP ARRFR No. 110 dated November 23, 2020. "On Approval of the Rules for Assessing the Level of Protection against Information Security Threats"
PP ARRFR No. 111 dated November 23, 2020. "On Approval of the Information Security Risk Assessment Methodology, Including the Procedure for Ranking Financial Organizations by the Degree of Exposure to Information Security Risks"

Printed by Books on Demand GmbH, Norderstedt / Germany